# 50 Great Irish Love Songs

Robert Gogan

Music Ireland

Published by Music Ireland, Achill Island, Co. Mayo, Ireland

www.greatirishballads.com

**"The Golden Jubilee":** copyright control
**"The Sally Gardens":** copyright control
**"She Moved Through The Fair"**: by kind permission of the Estate of Padraic Colum

Printed and packaged by Everbest Printing Company, China
Designed and compiled by Robert Gogan
Cover design by Ed McGinley, MGA Design Consultants, Dublin

**Photographs**
Front cover photographs courtesy of Bord Fáilte – The Irish Tourist Board
"Girl with sunlit hair" by Brian Lynch
"Sunset, Rossnowlagh, County Donegal" by Pat O'Dea
Back cover photograph "Musical Instrument Medley" by Declan O'Brien
Internal photographs:
Robert Gogan, Anne Tyrrell, Paul Jackson and as stated

**CD**
Recorded at Sonic Studios, Dublin.
Engineer: Al Cowan
Produced by Robert Gogan

**Musicians**
Sinéad Martin (Guitar/Vocals)
John Doyle (Vocals)
Roddy Gallagher (Guitar)
Robert Gogan (Guitar/Vocals)

ISBN    978 0 9550974 0 9

Earlsfort Terrace, Dublin. "The Kiss" by Ronan Gillespie

# Guitar chords used in this book

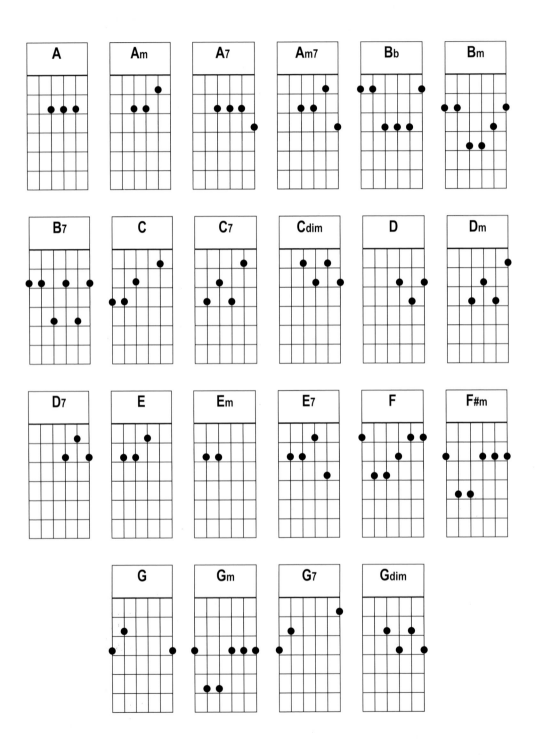

*We have just about enough religion to make us hate,*
*but not enough to make us love one another*
Jonathan Swift

*Put your hand on a stove for a minute and it seems like an hour;*
*sit with a pretty girl for an hour and it seems like a minute.*
*That's relativity*
Albert Einstein

*Remember that all through history the way of truth and love has always won.*
*There have been tyrants and murderers and for a time they seem invincible*
*but in the end, they always fall*
Mahatma Gandhi

*Nobody will ever win the battle of the sexes.*
*There's too much fraternising with the enemy*
Henry Kissinger

*Love me when I least deserve it, because that's when I really need it*
Swedish proverb

*He that falls in love with himself will have no rivals*
Benjamin Franklin

*Men always want to be a woman's first love;*
*women like to be a man's last romance*
Oscar Wilde

# 50 Great Irish Love Songs
## 3rd Edition

## Introduction

The Irish make great lovers, and these songs prove it!

In this book you have all you need to learn to play and sing some of the greatest Irish love songs ever written – the lyrics, guitar chords and simplified music score.

With the third edition of this book I've included additional information about many of the songs. My research brought me down many alleyways of folklore, history and legend and I hope that this has helped to bring some of the songs alive for you. I've also included some appropriate images of Ireland and other relevant photographs.

And what a magnificent selection of songs, from the haunting "Danny Boy" and "She Moved Through The Fair" to the beautiful "Mountains Of Mourne" and "Rose Of Tralee" and to the mischievous "German Clockwinder" and "Maids When You're Young" They're all here!

So enjoy these songs! Sing them! Change the words or music or timing if you feel something else works better for you! After all, that's what ballads are all about!

### A Big Thank You

There are many people who encouraged and helped me with this book. I would like to thank Trish Ryan, Sharon Murphy and Dec "I'll get this C diminished to work if it kills me" O'Brien for all of the practical help they gave me.

I would also like to give special thanks to Karen O'Mahony from the Mechanical Copyright Protection Society for the countless hours she spent trying to unravel the maze of copyright control on these songs. Without her help I doubt if this book would exist today. And also thanks to Michael Basinski from the State University at Buffalo for permission to use the image of the Joyces on their wedding day, Sandra McDermott of the National Library of Ireland for sourcing and organising the various permissions for other old photographs, Paul Jackson for permission to use several of his photographs, Laurette Kiernan for permission to reproduce Kitty Kiernan's image and the family of Pádraic Colum for permission to reproduce "She Moved Through The Fair".

In particular I wish to thank my wife Anne, not only for her encouragement and patience as I put this project together, but also for her dedicated research into the many different aspects of the stories in the book, and for sourcing many of the images.

### The CD

If you're not familiar with the particular melody of a song and can't read music the accompanying CD will provide you with the basic tune. The recordings are in the same key as they appear in the book which gives you the opportunity to play along with the CD if you wish.

**The Chorus**

If a song has a chorus it is printed in bold italics *like this*. Some songs start with a chorus and therefore it will be in the main body of the score. Others have the chorus after the first verse.

Choruses are great things – they are a 'law unto themselves'. You can add more in (and this normally depends on the number of verses the singer knows!), or take them out if you want to shorten the song. So do your own thing! Do it your way!

But above all, enjoy these songs! They are crying out to be sung!

I am indebted to the following publications and websites for facts, information and references:

*"The Poolbeg Book of Irish Ballads"* by Sean McMahon. Poolbeg Press
*"The Complete Guide to Celtic Music"* by June Skinner Sawyers. Aurum Press
*"Bird Life in Ireland"* by Don Conroy & Jim Wilson. The O'Brien Press
*"The Oxford Companion to Irish History"* edited by S.J. Connolly. Oxford University Press
*"AA Illustrated Road Book of Ireland"* The Automobile Association
*"Irish Ballads"* edited by Fleur Robertson. Gill & MacMillan
*"The Easter Rebellion"* by Max Caulfield. Gill & MacMillan
*"Harry Boland's Irish Revolution"* by David Fitzpatrick. Cork University Press
*"Robert Emmet - A Life"* by Patrick M. Geoghegan. Gill & MacMillan
*"Robert Emmet - The Making of a Legend"* by Marianne Elliott. Profile Books
*"Michael Collins"* by Tim Pat Coogan. Arrow Books
*"Michael Collins - The Lost Leader"* by Margery Forester. Sphere Books
*"Willie & Maud"* by Barry Shortall. The Collins Press
*"The Encyclopaedia of Ireland"*. General editor Brian Lalor. Gill & MacMillan
*"Sacred Ireland"* by Cary Meehan. Gothic Image Publications
*"Shanties from the Seven Seas"* by Stan Hugill. Mystic Seaport
www.contemplator.com
www.standingstones.com
www.mudcat.org
www.wikipedia.org

*Robert Gogan*
*2008*

# Thomas Moore (1779 - 1852)

*T*homas Moore was born in Dublin on May 28th, 1779, son of a shoemaker. He studied at Trinity College Dublin and was a friend of Robert Emmet who led a small and unsuccessful rebellion in Dublin in 1803 and was executed as a result - see page 51.

Moore was also acquainted with many of the United Irishmen and contributed to their newspaper, "The Press". Combining his compositions with popular Irish airs of the period he published his works in the famous collections entitled "Irish Melodies", but now more popularly known as "Moore's Irish Melodies" or "Moore's Melodies". There were ten volumes, the first appearing in 1807 and the final one with a supplement appearing in 1834. The "Irish Melodies" were immensely popular in Ireland and Britain. The ten volumes contained 130 songs.

Moore in his "Irish Melodies" was seeking a richer and more sophisticated audience for Irish songs and the first volume was dedicated to "the Nobility and Gentry of Ireland". He was attempting to portray a more peaceful side to Irish Nationalism and his ballads are a far cry from the blood-thirsty and rabble-rousing ballads which proliferated the streets and ale houses in the early 19th century.

There were two distinctly different attitudes among Irish people towards Moore's ballads. Some considered that he had achieved more to awaken the nationalistic spirit of Irishmen than the violent ballads more familiar to the Irish ear, while others regarded the "Irish Melodies" as whinging songs, bemoaning the downtrodden plight of Irish people while hanging on to the coat-tails of the oppressor pleading for mercy.

Some of Moore's ballads were reprinted on street ballad broadsides in the middle years of the nineteenth century, particularly such songs as "Let Erin Remember" and "The Minstrel Boy".

There are three of Moore's ballads in this book:-

**"Believe Me If All Those Endearing Young Charms"** *(page 53)*

**"The Last Rose Of Summer"** *(page 24)*

**"The Meeting Of The Waters"** *(page 58)*

College Green, Dublin   Thomas Moore statue

# Tristan and Isolde

*T*he legend of Tristan and Isolde has been told and retold in various stories and manuscripts throughout Europe down through the ages and is very much the ultimate tragic love story.

The character of Tristan may have been based on a Pictish prince named Drust who lived in the Highlands of Scotland in the 8th century.

Tristan, in the story, is the son of Rivalen and Blancheflor. Blancheflor gave birth to Tristan a short time after Rivalen had fallen in battle. She was inconsolable with grief over his death and spent three days in labour before giving birth. She named her new son Tristan because of the sorrow she had suffered during her labour.

Tristan was brought up well by Rivalen's followers. He was proficient at art and music and possessed all the skills required to be a nobleman. He eventually became a member of the court of King Mark of Cornwall. King Mark, a brother of Blancheflor, was unaware that Tristan was his nephew, but when he discovered the truth he was overjoyed and made him a knight.

In a fierce battle with one of King Mark's enemies, Morholt (an Irish Duke), Tristan received a wound which wouldn't heal. Morholt, who was slain in the battle, has previously informed Tristan that the only person who could heal his wounds was Queen Iseult in Ireland. Tristan decided to try his luck by going to Ireland to seek out a cure.

Queen Iseult produced the cure for Tristan's wounds and King Mark rejoiced at this news. During his convalescence Tristan became well acquainted with Queen Iseult's daughter, Isolde.

When he returned to Cornwall, Tristan became King Mark's closest companion.

Some time later Tristan returned to Ireland to try to persuade Isolde to return with him to marry King Mark, as the king was unwed and was therefore without a son to carry on the lineage. Isolde's mother persuaded her to do this, as she realised that the son from such a marriage would become the ruler of Ireland and Cornwall.

Before Tristan and Isolde left Ireland to return to Cornwall to King Mark, Queen Iseult prepared a love potion. She entrusted this potion to Isolde's maid, Brangwain, and instructed her to administer it to her daughter and King Mark before the wedding because she feared that Isolde might change her mind when she realised that King Mark was a much older man.

The love potion was concealed in a bottle of wine and on the journey back to Cornwall Tristan and Isolde became thirsty and drank the love potion, thinking it to be wine.

They fell instantly and madly in love.

When Brangwain realised what had happened she informed the two lovers. Notwithstanding Tristan's feelings for Isolde, he knew that she must fulfil her commitment and proceed with the marriage to his uncle, King Mark.

Isolde and King Mark were married as planned. King Mark fell deeply in love with Isolde as soon as he laid eyes on the beautiful maiden, but her feelings lay elsewhere.

No matter how much Tristan tried to remain faithful to his uncle, his feelings for Isolde were too strong for him to resist. Isolde was also in the same predicament. They availed of every opportunity to meet and were constantly making plans to meet in private so that they could enjoy each other's love. It wasn't too long before King Mark discovered the liaison between Tristan and his wife. He banished Tristan from his kingdom. Tristan left Cornwall and served various different kings and fought many battles. He eventually settled in Brittany. All during this time he could not banish Isolde from his mind or heart.

He eventually married a girl who, ironically, was also called Isolde and was known as Isolde of the White Hands. However, he still could not rid himself of his feelings for his Irish Isolde. For this reason Tristan never consummated his marriage with his wife.

Eventually Tristan decided to travel back to Cornwall to see his beloved Isolde once again. When they met, she was angry that he had married, but soon forgave him. Her feelings for Tristan also hadn't changed.

However Tristan knew that he had no choice but to eventually return to his wife in Brittany.

On the return journey to Brittany Tristan became embroiled with one of his enemies and received a mortal wound. He knew that only his beloved Isolde could heal him. He sent a messenger to fetch Isolde. If Isolde agreed to return with him, the messenger was to hoist a white sail on his boat. If Isolde was not with him, the messenger was to hoist a black sail.

When Isolde heard from the messenger that her beloved Tristan was near death she immediately agreed to return with him.

However, when Tristan's wife, Isolde, saw the ship with the white sails, she told him that the ship was in fact showing black sails. Tristan, heartbroken, felt that there was no point in trying to hold onto his life and he died.

When Isolde landed with the messenger in Brittany she rushed to her lover's side, only to realise that he had died just moments before. She wrapped her arms around him and her life quickly drained out of her. She died, in her beloved's arms, of a broken heart.

# Index by Song Title & CD Track

# Index by First Line

Dooniver Beach, Achill Island

This song is printed in the collection "Irish Country Songs" (1909) edited by Herbert Hughes where he states that this is an old song which originated in the west of Ireland. Hughes says that in the counties of Galway and Clare the ballad is usually sung in alternate verses of Irish and English.

A longer version of this ballad is said to exist in Scotland. Mardyke is an area in Cork City in the south of Ireland and the "hall" referred to in the ballad is probably St. Francis' Hall where many's a good dance or 'hop' took place over the years!

The song enjoyed a recent revival through a recording of it by The Chieftans for their album "Tears Of Stone" (1999) which featured The Corrs.

The song itself was released as a single and received significant airplay throughout Ireland.

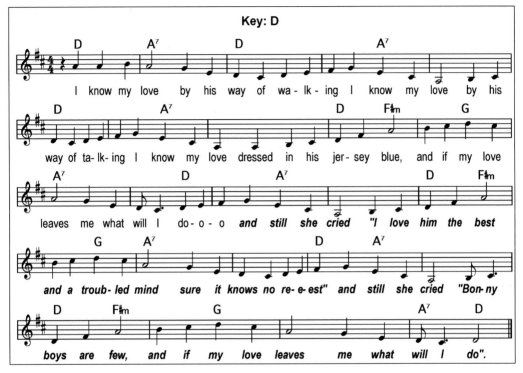

I know my love by his way of wa-lk-ing I know my love by his way of ta-lk-ing I know my love dressed in his jer-sey blue, and if my love leaves me what will I do-o-o *and still she cried "I love him the best and a troub-led mind sure it knows no re-e-est" and still she cried "Bon-ny boys are few, and if my love leaves me what will I do".*

There is a dance house down in Mardyke
'Tis there my true love goes every night
He takes a strange girl upon his knee
And don't you think now that vexes me?
*Chorus*

If my love knew I could wash and wring
If my love knew I could weave and spin
I'd make a suit of the finest kind
But the want of money leaves me behind
*Chorus*

I know my love is an arrant rover
I know my love roams the wide world over
In some foreign town he may chance to tarry
And some foreign maid he will surely marry
*Chorus*

Glenade Lake, Leitrim

# Carrickfergus

This old and well known ballad acquired renewed popularity through a recent recording of it by Irish singer Van Morrison. It was originally known as "The Sick Young Lover".
The song in its present form may have evolved from two separate songs which would explain why some of the lyrics don't quite make sense. A broadside containing both English and Irish verses was published in Cork in or around 1830. George Petrie in his "Ancient Music Of Ireland" (1855) also published a tune called "The Young Lady" which includes many of the words of this ballad.

In the US Library of Congress 'Music For The Nation' section there are records of a song called "Sweet Maggie Gordon", published by a Mrs. Pauline Lieder in New York in 1880, and arranged by Mr. Ned Straight. The verses of the song bear a remarkable resemblance to this song, but the chorus is very similar to another song in this book - "Peggy Gordon" (page 82)
The town of Carrickfergus in County Antrim stands on the shores of Belfast Lough about 11 miles from Belfast, the capital of Northern Ireland. It is a picturesque port in an old world setting.

My childhood days bring sad reflections of happy times spent long ago
My boyhood friends and my own relations have all passed on now like the melting snow
So I'll spend my days in endless roving; soft is the grass, my bed is free
Ah, to be back now in Carrickfergus, on that long road down to the sea

Now in Kilkenny, it is reported there are marble stones as black as ink
With gold and silver I would support her but I'll sing no more now till I get a drink
I'm drunk today and I'm seldom sober, a handsome rover from town to town
Ah, but I'm sick now and my days are over, so come all ye young lads and lay me down

# The Rose Of Tralee

This song is the county anthem of County Kerry and was written by William Pembroke Mulchinock (1820 - 1864).

The Mulchinocks were a fairly prosperous family living in Tralee and William fell in love with Mary O'Connor, the daughter of one of the family's servants. His parents were not at all happy with this liaison and young William was quickly sent abroad for fear that his affections might grow even stronger. Following a spell in France and India William returned to Tralee. Tradition has it that on his arrival back in Tralee he met a funeral party coming down the street. On making enquiries he was told that the deceased was his beloved Mary O'Connor, who had died from the disease of Consumption. William wrote this ballad in her memory, using a local tune about the nearby Ballymullan Castle as his model.

William Mulchinock wrote many poems for various Irish journals, among them "The Nation" newspaper. He left for New York in 1849 and achieved considerable success as a writer of lyrics. In 1851 he published a collection, entitled "The Ballads and Songs of W.P. Mulchinock", which oddly enough, does not contain "The Rose of Tralee".

He returned to Tralee in 1855 and died there in 1864.

The Rose of Tralee is now one of the best known and loved of all Irish ballads at home and abroad. Its popularity and endurance was assisted in no small way by a fine recording of the song by the Irish tenor John McCormack many years ago.

Tralee, the capital of County Kerry is situated near the mouth of Tralee Bay in the south-west of Ireland and is about 20 miles from Killarney. Tralee is home to a major international festival, the 'Rose of Tralee' Festival, which celebrates the beauty of the Irish Colleen and takes place every August. Tralee also has a fine racecourse and the Tralee Racing Festival is held annually at the end of August. Both festivals are well worth a visit!

If you're in Tralee, take some time out to visit the Kerry County Museum in the centre of the town. I found it to be a most interesting museum, where interactive media and reconstructions stand side-by-side with treasures dating from the Stone and Bronze Age right up to the present day. Also in the same building you have "Kerry in Colour" - a panoramic multi-image audio-visual tour of County Kerry, and "Geraldine Tralee" where you are transported back 600 years and experience a day in the life of a medieval town, complete with sounds and smells.

Just outside the town is Blennerville Windmill - a living reminder of Ireland's rich industrial heritage. It features in the Guinness Book of Records as "the largest working windmill in these islands".

The cool shades of evening their mantles were spreading
And Mary, all smiling, sat list'ning to me
The moon through the valley her pale rays was shedding
When I won the heart of the Rose of Tralee
*Chorus*

In the far fields of India 'mid war's dreadful thunders
Her voice was a solace and comfort to me
But the chill hand of death has now rent us asunder
I'm lonely tonight for the Rose of Tralee
*Chorus*

Selling hats in Tralee

6

# William Butler Yeats and Maud Gonne

Courtesy of National Library of Ireland

W B Yeats (1865 - 1939) is regarded as one of the greatest of the Anglo-Irish poets. His mother's family were merchants from County Sligo - hence his many associations with the county. He spent his formative years in London, Dublin and Sligo.

His first works were published in the 1880's and his poetry drew extensively from Gaelic literature and Sligo folklore. Yeats mobilised the nationalist literary groups at the time into a movement for a national artistic revival. This culminated in the foundation of the Irish Literary Theatre, later to be called the Abbey Theatre, in Dublin.

Yeats was awarded the Nobel Prize for Literature in 1923. He served in the Irish Free State as a Senator from 1922 to 1928.

He died in France in 1939 and in 1948 his remains were returned to Ireland and re-interred in the quiet graveyard in Drumcliffe, County Sligo. The epitaph on his tombstone ("Cast a cold Eye on Life, on Death. Horseman pass by") has been the subject of many's a lengthy discussion among Irish literary scholars down through the years.

Maud Gonne (1866 - 1953) was born in England. She was sent to Paris to be educated following her mother's death. Her father, a British army officer, was posted to Dublin in 1882 and Maud accompanied him and remained with him in Dublin until his death in 1886.

Following a relationship with a French journalist she returned to Ireland and in 1903 married John McBride and bore him a son, Seán. She later separated from her husband and returned to France. When John McBride was executed for his part in the 1916 Rising Maud returned to Ireland and fought and campaigned tirelessly on social and nationalist issues. She died in 1953.

Yeats first met Maud Gonne in January 1889 when she visited the Yeats family home in London. She was an actress and a woman of considerable social standing, tall, confident and beautiful. At first the twenty-three year old Yeats was fascinated by her and they spent a great deal of time together over the next nine days. By the time Maud was leaving London Yeats was uncontrollably and totally in love with her.

Yeats used to ponder the curious situation in which he found himself - a quiet reserved and academic poet in love with an outspoken ardent Nationalist. At this time much of his poetry was influenced by his emotions towards Maud and in 1902 she played the leading role at the Abbey Theatre in his play "Cathleen Ní Houlihan".

Unaware of her clandestine love life in Paris, Yeats proposed marriage to Maud for the first time in 1891 but was refused. He vowed to continue his courtship of her in the hope that he'd eventually persuade her to marry him. Alas, this was never to be.

Courtesy of National Library of Ireland

He continued to write poetry to, and about Maud and his love became the obsession of his life. He regularly proposed marriage and, regularly, was rejected.

He was outraged when in 1903 she married Major John McBride. He tried desperately to dissuade her. The marriage lasted a short time and ended in an acrimonious separation.

Throughout this time Yeats and Maud were in communication in, what she described, a platonic relationship. In 1909 she told Yeats in a letter that she considered that they had a spiritual union which would outlive them in this life.

Yeats was so obsessed with Maud at this time that he actively considered marrying her daughter Iseult, whom she had during her love affair in Paris.

Following the execution of Major John McBride in 1916 Yeats proposed to Maud for the last time and was rejected once again. He then proposed to Iseult (who was 22 at the time and he was 51) and, after a period of indecision by her, she also declined.

Within a month Yeats married Georgie Hyde-Lees. His heart, however, still belonged to Maud. There followed several liaisons with other women until, finally, in 1908, Yeats and Maud Gonne consummated their relationship in Paris. Their relationship, however, did not develop after their one night of passion together and Yeats kept his one true love in the forefront of his life, dreams and work for the rest of his life.

Yeats is buried in Drumcliffe cemetery in County Sligo and Maud Gonne in buried in the Republican plot at Glasnevin Cemetery, Dublin.

This is a beautiful Irish love song, the lyrics of which were written by William Butler Yeats and published in his collection of poems "Crossways" (1889).

The song is printed in the collection "Irish Country Songs" (1909) edited by Herbert Hughes.

When Yeats was in the town of Ballisodare in County Sligo he heard a local man singing a plaintive folk tune called "The Maids of the Mountain Shore" and this inspired him to write the poem. There was once a row of thatched cottages near the mills at Ballisodare and each of them had a sally garden attached. Yeats considered this to be an ideal place for lovers to meet - hence the song.

Sally (or Salley) comes from the Irish word for willow. Willow rods (osiers) were used in basket-making and for providing scallops for thatching. They were grown specially for those purposes.

County Sligo is situated on the north-east coast of Ireland. County Sligo and parts of adjoining County Leitrim are widely referred to as 'the Yeats Country'.

Key: D

'Twa-s down by the Sal - l - y Gar - dens m - y love a - nd I did meet. She - e passed th - e Sal - l - y Gard - ens wi - th lit - tl - e snow white feet. She bid me take love e - as - y as the leaves gro- w on th - e tree. Bu - t I be - ing young a - nd fool- ish wi - th her di - d not a - gree.

In a field down by the river my love and I did stand
And on my leaning shoulder she laid her snow-white hand
She bid me take life easy as the grass grows on the weirs
But I was young and foolish and now am full of tears

*(Repeat first verse)*

Yeats' grave, Drumcliffe Cemetery, Sligo

# The Hills Of Kerry

*(Verses and chorus have the same melody)*

Although this is a well known Irish ballad and is particularly popular in County Kerry, there doesn't appear to be any information available as to its origin.

County Kerry is situated in the south-west of Ireland in the province of Munster. It is bordered by Counties Limerick and Cork and has some of the most popular tourist attractions in Ireland - the lakes of Killarney and the towns of Tralee, Dingle,

Killarney and Kenmare.

The tip of the Dingle Peninsula is the most westerly point of the mainland of Ireland.

Tralee is Kerry's administrative town.

There are two other songs in this book based in Tralee - "The Rose Of Tralee" (page 4) and "The Golden Jubilee" (page 21)

The noble and the brave
Have departed from our shore
They've gone off to a foreign land
Where the mighty canyons roar
No more they'll see the shamrock
Or the hills so dear to me
Or hear the small birds singing
All around you, sweet Tralee
*Chorus*

No more the sun will shine
On that blessed harvest morn
Or hear the reaper singing
In the fields of golden corn
There's a balm for every woe
And a cure for every pain
But the pretty smile of my darling girl
I'll never see again
*Chorus*

**I Never Will Marry**

*(Verses and chorus have the same melody)*

There doesn't appear to be any information available about the origins or history of this song.

Linda Ronstadt recorded it with Dolly Parton on her 1977 album "Simple Dreams". Lester Flatt and Earl Scruggs of The Foggy Mountain Boys also recorded a version of it.

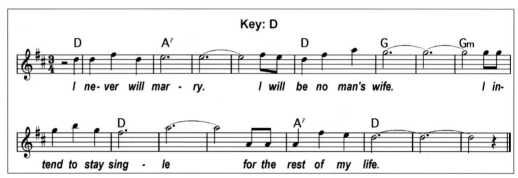

**Key: D**

I ne-ver will mar-ry. I will be no man's wife. I in-tend to stay sing - le for the rest of my life.

One day as I rambled down by the seashore
The wind it did whistle and the waters did roar
I heard a young maiden make a pitiful cry
She sounded so lonesome at the waters nearby
*Chorus*

"The shells in the ocean will be my death bed
May the fish in the waters swim over my head
My love's gone and left me; he's the one I adore
I never will see him, no never, no more"
*Chorus*

She plunged her fair body in the water so deep
She closed her pretty blue eyes in the waters to sleep
And that lonesome maiden and her pitiful cries
Can be heard from the ocean to the heavenly skies
*Chorus*

Jewish wedding in bygone days. Courtesy of National Library of Ireland

This song was written by James Thornton and first published in 1898. The cover of the sheet music states that it was 'sung with great success by Bonnie Thornton'.

James Thornton (1861 - 1938) was an American composer and lyricist. Born in Liverpool, he emigrated to the United States in 1869 and became an American citizen in 1931. Thornton started his career in Boston as a "singing waiter" and then became successful in music halls throughout the US, appearing with his wife, Bonnie. His last public appearance was in 1934 at the Forrest Theatre in New York.

One of the best known versions of the song was recorded by Al Jolson in 1929 and it was also a hit for Perry Como in 1947.

This gentle love song became very popular in Ireland following a recording of it by the Irish folk group The Furey Brothers, who reached no. 14 in the UK Charts with the song in October 1981.

Last night I dreamt I held your hand in mine
And once again you were my happy bride
I kissed you as I did in 'Auld Lang Syne'
As to the church we wandered side by side
*Chorus*

Newgrange, Meath

**Red Is The Rose**

*(Verses and chorus have the same melody)*

This is a simple and charming Irish ballad sung to the air of the Scottish tune "Loch Lomond".
Tommy Makem recorded a version of this song on his album, "Songbag" (1990). In the sleeve notes he says that he learned the song from his mother, Sarah.

I've contributed a verse of my own to this song ("But time passes on, etc").

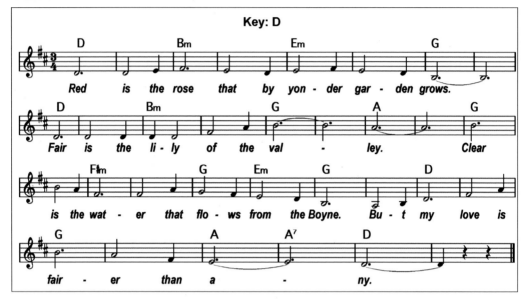

Come over the hills my bonny Irish lass
Come over the hills to your darling
You choose the rose, love, and I will make the vow
And I'll be your true love forever
*Chorus*

'Twas down by Killarney's green woodlands that we strayed
The moon and the stars they were shining
The moon shone its beams through her locks of golden hair
She swore she would love me forever
*Chorus*

But time passes on and my darling girl is gone
She's gone and she's met with another
I'm full of regret but my heart will ne'er forget
That once she was truly my lover
*Chorus*

It's not for the parting that my sister pains
It's not for the grief of my mother
It's all for the loss of my bonny Irish lass
That my heart is broken forever
*Chorus*

This popular ballad was also known as "Fare Thee Well, My Own True Love" and is widely sung on both sides of the Irish Sea.
For Irish emigrants Liverpool was the natural port of embarkation, mainly because it served the necessary shipping lines and therefore a larger choice of destinations.

Bob Dylan adapted the song and retitled it "Farewell", although it has never been officially released.
It has been recorded by many different artists, including The Dubliners, Ewan MacColl, and The Pogues.

I am sailing upon a Yankee sailing ship, Davy Crockett is her name
And her captain's name is Burgess, and they say she is a floating shame
*Chorus*

I have shipped with Burgess once before and I think I know him well
If a man's a sailor he can get along; if not then he is sure in hell
*Chorus*

Oh the sun is on the harbour love, and I wish I could remain
For I know it will be a long long time e'er I see you once again
*Chorus*

Killybegs Harbour, Donegal

'Donnelly's Hollow", The Curragh, Kildare
On this site a boxing match took place in 1815 in which the Irish Dan Donnelly defeated the English champion,
George Cooper.  Such was the euphoria at the time that Donnelly's footsteps were preserved on leaving the scene.

*(The last verse has only two lines - these are sung to the melody of the last two lines of the verse)*

This beautiful ballad appears in George Petrie's collection, "Ancient Music Of Ireland" (1855), both under the present title and also that of "The Winter It Is Past".

Petrie states that a printed version of this ballad is in "The Scots Musical Museum", published in Edinburgh by the collector James Johnson in 1787 and that it also appears in the Scottish collection "Caledonian Pocket Companion" edited by James Oswald (c. 1750) under the title "The Winter It Is Past". But the ballad was also collected in Ireland by Patrick Joyce, from the singing of Kate Cudmore, 'a peasant of Glenroe in the parish of Ardpatrick', County Limerick.

So the debate continues as to the origin of this song - Scotland or Ireland. Petrie believes that the Irish argument is 'decidedly the stronger'.

This ballad is reputed to be about a girl (Scottish or Irish?), heartbroken for her beloved who is an English soldier based in the Curragh military camp in County Kildare. She is so sorrowful that she contemplates disguising herself and enlisting in the army so that she could be with him.

The Curragh is an undulating open plain of about 5,000 acres which lies immediately east of Kildare town, about 30 miles south-east of Dublin. It derives its name from the Irish word 'An Currach' which means 'The Racecourse'. The magnificent racecourse at The Curragh is the venue for many race meetings, including the Irish Derby.

The Curragh military camp has been in existence for centuries and the British administration established a permanent military base there in 1854. A section of the Irish army is now based there.

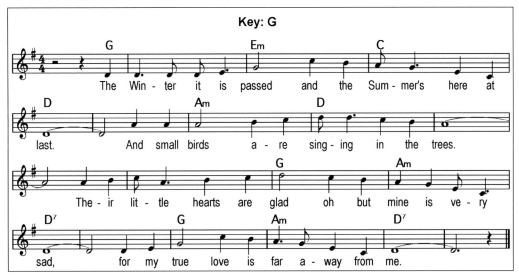

All you that are in love and cannot it remove
I pity all the pain that you endure
For experience lets me know that your hearts are full of woe
It's a woe that no mortal can endure

The rose upon the briar and the water running free
Gives joy to the linnet and the bee
Their little hearts are blessed but mine is not at rest
For my true love is far away from me

A livery I will wear and I'll straighten back my hair
In velvet so green I will appear
And it's then I will repair to the Curragh of Kildare
For it's there I'll find tidings of my dear

*(Repeat last two lines)*

**Love Is Teasing**

This is a well-known and oft-sung ballad in Irish sessions and has been recorded by many balladeers, including The Dubliners on their album "The Dubliners" (1964)

Marianne Faithful sings a lovely version of this ballad on The Chieftain's album "The Long Black Veil" (1995)

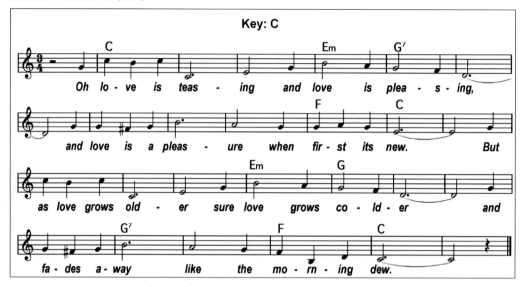

Key: C

Oh lo - ve is teas - ing and love is plea - s - ing, and love is a pleas - ure when fir - st its new. But as love grows old - er sure love grows co - ld - er and fa - des a - way like the mo - rn - ing dew.

I left my father, I left my mother
I left all my sisters and brothers too
I left all my friends and my own relations
I left them all for to follow you
*Chorus*

And love and porter make a young man older
And love and whiskey make an old man grey
What can't be cured, love, must be endured, love
And now I am bound for Americay
*Chorus*

The sweetest apple is soonest rotten
The hottest love is the soonest cold
What can't be cured, love, must be endured, love
And now I am bound for Americay
*Chorus*

I wish, I wish, I wish in vain
I wish that I was a maid again
But a maid again I can never be
Till apples grow on an ivy tree
*Chorus*

Detail from O'Connell Monument,
O'Connell Street, Dublin

This song is a traditional children's skipping game song and there appears to be no information in relation to its origins. There is a ballad very similar to it, called "The Wind". Belfast is the capital city of Northern Ireland and is situated in the north east of Ireland.

The song was a favourite in any live set of The Clancy Brothers and was recorded by them for their album "The Boys Won't Leave The Girls Alone" (1962)

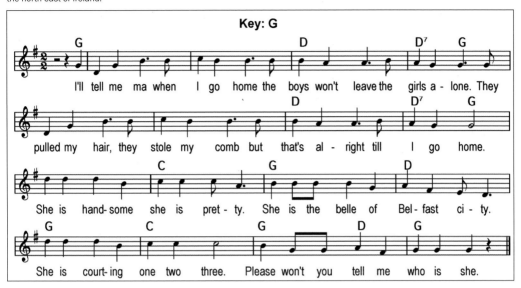

**Key: G**

I'll tell me ma when I go home the boys won't leave the girls a - lone. They

pulled my hair, they stole my comb but that's al - right till I go home.

She is hand-some she is pret - ty. She is the belle of Bel - fast ci - ty.

She is court-ing one two three. Please won't you tell me who is she.

Albert Mooney says he loves her
All the boys are fighting for her
They rap at the door and they ring at the bell
Saying "O my true love are you well"
Out she comes as white as snow
Rings on her fingers bells on her toes
Jenny Murray says she'll die
If she doesn't get the fella with the roving eye

Let the wind and the rain and the hail blow high
And the snow come tumbling from the sky
She's as nice as apple pie
She'll get her own lad by and by
When she gets a lad of her own
She won't tell her ma when she goes home
But let them all come as they will
It's Albert Mooney she loves still

*(Repeat first verse)*

Fitzwilliam Square, Dublin

# Michael Collins and Kitty Kiernan

*M*ichael Collins (1890 - 1922) was a revolutionary nationalist and one of the most important figures in the Irish struggle for self-rule.

Born in County Cork, he emigrated to London and

Courtesy of National Library of Ireland

worked in the Post Office at the age of fifteen. He returned to Dublin and immersed himself in the struggle for Irish freedom. He took part in the 1916 Rising, fighting alongside Pádraig Pearse in the GPO in Dublin.

Following a brief internment along with other Irish Revolutionaries after the failed Rising he returned to Ireland and became leader of the Irish Republican Brotherhood, a covert revolutionary organisation.

When Éamon De Valera travelled to America to promote the Irish Cause, Collins became de facto leader of the Irish Revolutionary Movement. As director of organisation and intelligence for the IRB he waged a skilful war against the British administration in Ireland, pre-empting many of their movements and disrupting their plans through his wide network of loyal spies and ruthless gunmen.

He devised and employed a system of guerilla warfare against the British and he is acknowledged as the originator of this particular method of combat which has been used extensively throughout the world.

By 1920 the British authorities were devoting an enormous amount of effort and energy into capturing Collins but without any success, notwithstanding the fact that they had offered a reward of £10,000 for information leading to his capture.

Following on the many successes of Collins against the British administration the Anglo-Irish Treaty was finally signed between the British and Irish representatives in 1921. Michael Collins was one of the envoys for the Irish Treaty Delegation. When Collins signed the Treaty he wrote to his beloved Kitty Kiernan, saying that he felt that he had just signed his own death warrant - a comment which was ominously close to reality.

A bitter civil war broke out in Ireland between the pro-treaty and anti-treaty factions, with Collins acting as Commander-in-Chief of the Government forces (pro-treaty). Éamon de Valera, his former ally and comrade, was leader of the anti-treaty forces.

Government forces were gaining the upper hand in the civil war and in 1922 Collins travelled to Cork for a secret meeting with de Valera to see if they could find a compromise and end to the bloodshed. On the journey Collins' convoy was ambushed on a narrow dirt road in the quiet townland of Bealnablath in Cork and he was fatally wounded in the ensuing gunfight.

At the funeral of Arthur Griffith a week before his death, Collins was heard to say "Why has Ireland always lost its leaders when it had the greatest need of them?"

By signing the Anglo-Irish Treaty in 1921 he had indeed signed his own death warrant.

Kitty (Catherine Bridget) Kiernan (1892 - 1945) was born in Granard in County Longford into a comfortable merchant-class environment. The Kiernan family owned several businesses in the locality and Kitty's childhood was a happy and contented one.

By kind permission of Laurette Kiernan

Kitty met Michael Collins in 1917 during the by-election campaign in County Longford when he and his loyal comrade Harry Boland were staying in the area.

Both men were taken by her charm and vitality and there commenced an intense ménage-a-trois (which was never discouraged by Kitty) which resulted in Collins eventually winning her heart.

Boland was deeply in love with Kitty and was devastated when she informed him that she had chosen Collins. Indeed Boland, and many of their mutual friends, were convinced that Kitty's affections were very much leaning towards him and he was convinced that Kitty and himself would be engaged to be married by the year's end.

When Boland learned of Kitty's engagement to Collins he wrote her a curt two line letter of congratulations, in sharp contrast to the lyrical and colourful letters to her of former times.

There is no doubt that Kitty's choice of Collins over Boland put enormous strain on the two men's relationship.

Collins visited Kitty in Granard at every opportunity. However, his political activities caused him to be absent from her sometimes for quite a while and the couple compensated for this absence by engaging in a prolific amount of letter-writing.

Collins and Kitty kept up extensive correspondence and he wrote to her on a daily basis while in London during the Anglo-Irish Treaty negotiations. (These letters are the subject of a book called "In Great Haste" (1983) by Leon O'Broin.)

The letters reveal the intimacy between the couple and also reflect the enormous pressure on the shoulders of Collins as he tried to perform a balancing act to satisfy all factions in the complex political environment. In many of his letters he writes that he is too weary and exhausted to complete a proper letter. In many of her letters she passionately expresses her deep love for him and is worried at the burdens on his shoulders.

It appears that Collins and Kitty considered the question of marriage during his stay in London and a date was set for October 1922.

During these troubled days the couple had at least one opportunity, in June 1922, to consummate their love

for each other and, after the event, she wrote ecstatically about it to him. Collins in his letters to Kitty is more reserved and cautious, being well aware that his correspondence could fall into the wrong hands. He advised Kitty to be careful and vigilant when sending letters to him and to be aware that they could be intercepted.

Following the shooting of Collins at Bealnablath Kitty was utterly disconsolate with grief. She spent her days reading and re-reading his letters to her.

In 1925 she married Felix Cronin, a Quartermaster General in the Irish army. But Collins was never far from her thoughts and emotions. She hung a large portrait of her former lover in the living-room of their house, and called her second son, Michael Collins Cronin.

She died in 1945 following a lengthy illness and is buried in Glasnevin Cemetery, Dublin, not far from the grave of her beloved Michael Collins.

Memorial to Michael Collins, Bealnablath, Cork

# My Singing Bird

The lark (or to use its official name 'Skylark', or alauda arvensis) is a very common bird in Ireland. It is estimated that over one million skylarks breed in Ireland each year. Their favourite habitats are the open country and coastal dunes. They make their nests on the ground, usually under clumps of tall grass. They often perch and sing on fence posts. One of the great characteristics of skylarks is their practice of flying at high altitude, especially over stubble fields where they find most of their food - cereal grain and insects.

The lark is one of the first birds to be heard in the morning in open countryside - hence it has earned the reputation as a 'symbol' of the morning and the dawn of a new day. Its continuous song consists of a constant jumble of twittering, chirping and warbling sounds, often including the imitation of

other song birds.

It sings as it ascends into the heavens and hovers on fluttering wings, sometimes until it is almost out of sight.

If you want to keep your eyes open to spot skylarks their main features are sandy brown upper parts, streaked with dark brown. They have white outer tail feathers with a thin white trailing edge to their wings, visible only when open. Their underside consists of a white belly, buff breast with dark streaking heaviest on the sides. Their bills are pale, short and stubby. They have long legs, pale pink in colour with a very long claw on the hind toe.

If disturbed on the ground they will usually flutter off a short distance and land in the long grass.

There is another song in this book relating to the skylark. See "The Lark In The Morning" - page 35.

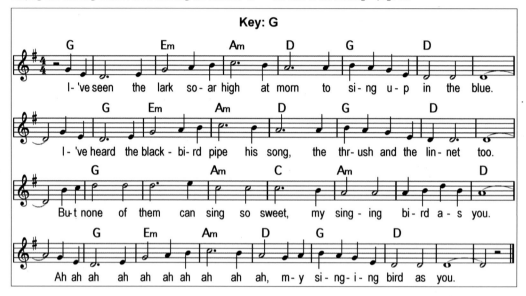

If I could lure my singing bird down from its own cosy nest
If I could catch my singing bird I'd warm it upon my breast
And in my heart my singing bird would sing itself to rest
Ah, ah, ah, ah, ah, ah, ah, ah, ah, ah, would sing itself to rest

A singing bird on the Great Blasket Island

*(Verses and chorus have the same melody)*

This is a charming ballad about a Kerry couple growing old together.

Unfortunately there doesn't appear to be any information available as to its origins.

Tralee is the 'county town' of County Kerry and the gateway to the Dingle Peninsula, situated in the south-west of Ireland. There's another ballad in this book about a girl from Tralee. See "The Rose Of Tralee" - page 4.

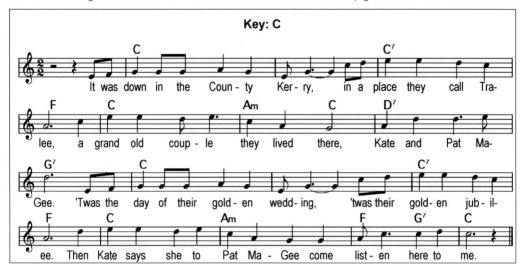

Key: C

It was down in the Coun - ty Ker - ry, in a place they call Tra-lee, a grand old coup - le they lived there, Kate and Pat Ma-Gee. 'Twas the day of their gold - en wedd- ing, 'twas their gold- en jub - il- ee. Then Kate says she to Pat Ma - Gee come list - en here to me.

*Put on your old knee britches and your coat of emerald green*
*Take off that hat me darling Pat, put on your old cáibin\**
*For today's our Golden Wedding and I'll have you all to know*
*Just how we looked when we were wed fifty years ago*

Oh well do I remember how we danced on the village green
You held me in your arms dear Pat and called me your colleen
Your hair was like a raven's wing but now it's turning grey
Come over here my sweetheart dear and hear what I've to say
*Chorus*

Oh well do I remember when first I was your bride
In the little chapel on the hill where we stood side by side
Of good friends we've had plenty, of troubles we've had few
Come over here my sweetheart dear and here's what you must do
*Chorus*

*Pronounced "cawbeen" (cloth cap)

# The Mountains Of Mourne

This song was written by Percy French (1854 - 1920).
He is reputed to have written it in 1896 on a very clear day when he could see the Mountains of Mourne from the Hill of Howth in north Dublin. He sent the lyrics to his friend and colleague, Houston Collison (on the back of a postcard!), and Collison set them to the air of the song "Carrigdhoun". "Carrigdhoun" is a very popular ballad in Cork, written by the Cork merchant Denny Lane (b. 1818). and first published in 'The Nation' newspaper in 1845.
William Percy French was born on May 1st 1854 in Cloonyquin, County Roscommon, in the mid-west of Ireland. He was reared in comfortable circumstances, educated at upmarket English schools and eventually at Trinity College Dublin. He certainly could not be described as a model student at Trinity College for he established the record during his 'studies' for the student who took the longest time to obtain a degree!
While most of French's songs are humorous and entertaining they never ridicule, but show a warm and genuine love and affection for the Irish country folk about whom he wrote. Other songs of his include "Are Ye Right There Michael", "Sweet Marie" and "Phil The Fluther's Ball".
This song is about a lonely Irish emigrant working in London and writing a letter to his beloved in Ireland.
Apart from writing many well-remembered and popular 'drawing-room' songs Percy French was also a fine landscape painter. Today his watercolours command high prices at art auctions.
The Mountains of Mourne are situated in County Down, in the north-east of Ireland. This mountain range, the highest in Northern Ireland, is dominated by Slieve Donard, at 2,796 feet. In clear weather the Welsh and English Lake District mountains can be seen from its peaks, as well as the Isle of Arran and the Isle of Man.
The American folk-rock artist, Don McLean, recorded a fine version of this ballad which he called "Mountains O'Mourne" on his album "Playin Favourites" (1989).

I believe that when writing a wish you expressed
As to how the young ladies of London were dressed
Well, if you'll believe me, when asked to a ball
Sure they don't wear a top to their dresses at all
Oh I've seen them myself and you could not in truth
Say if they were bound for a ball or a bath
Don't be starting them fashions now, Mary mo chroí*
Where the Mountains of Mourne sweep down to the sea

I've seen England's King from the top of a bus
Sure I never knew him but he means to know us
And though by the Saxon we once were oppressed
Still I cheered, God forgive me, I cheered with the rest
And now that he's visited Erin's green shore
We'll be much better friends than we've been heretofore
When we've got all we want we're as quiet as can be
Where the Mountains of Mourne sweep down to the sea

You remember young Peter O'Loughlin, of course
Well now he is here at the head of the Force
I met him today; I was crossing the Strand
And he stopped the whole street with one wave of his hand
And as we stood talking of days that were gone
The whole population of London looked on
But for all his great powers he's wishful like me
To be back where the dark Mourne sweeps down to the sea

There's beautiful girls here; oh never you mind
With beautiful shapes Nature never designed
And lovely complexions; all roses and cream
But O'Loughlin remarked with regard to the same
That if at those roses you venture to sip
The colour might all come away on your lip
So I'll wait for the wild rose that's waiting for me
Where the Mountains of Mourne sweep down to the sea

*Pronounced "cree" (my beloved)

The Mountains of Mourne

# The Last Rose Of Summer

This ballad was written in 1805 by the great Irish songwriter, Thomas Moore (1779 - 1852).
It was set to the old Irish air "The Young Man's Dream" which was also known as "The Groves Of Blarney".
Sarah Brightman recorded the song for an album entitled "The Trees They Grow So High"(1988), a collection of folksongs arranged by Benjamin Britten.
For further details about Thomas Moore and his songs see the Additional Notes at the front of this book.

**Key: C**

'Tis the last ro-se o-f sum - mer le-ft bloom - i-ng all a-lone.

All her love - l - y co-m-pan - ions a-re fad - e-d a-nd gone.

N-o flow - er of her kind - red, n-o ro - se - bud is nigh

to re - flect ba-ck h-er blush - es a-nd give si-gh f-or sigh.

I'll not leave thee, thou alone one, to pine on the stem
Since the lovely are sleeping go sleep, thou, with them
Thus kindly I scatter thy leaves o'er the bed
Where thy mates of the garden lie scentless and dead

So soon may I follow when friendships decay
And from love's shining circle the gems drop away
When true hearts lie withered and fond ones are flown
Oh who would inhabit this bleak world alone!

Ballad session
Temple Bar, Dublin

The lyrics of this ballad were translated from Irish by George Petrie and appear along with the air (in 4/4 timing) in his "Ancient Music of Ireland" (1855). The title of the ballad in Petrie's book is "The Pearl Of The White Breast". Petrie acknowledges that he obtained the words and music from a Mr. Eugene Curry of County Clare who was of the opinion that the song did not originate in County Clare but rather somewhere else on the west coast of Ireland. Petrie confesses, however, that in his own musical research in the west of Ireland he had never come across the air.

There is also an air and some lyrics which appear in "A General Collection of Ancient Irish Music" by Edward Bunting (1796) under the title "The Pearl Of The White Breast" but neither the melody nor lyrics relate to this version of the song.

A great version of this ballad was recorded in 1991 by the Irish folk group, The Wolfe Tones, on their album "Let The People Sing".

Oh thou blooming milk-white dove to whom I have aimed my love
Do not ever thus reprove my constancy
There are maidens would be mine with a wealth in land and kine
If my heart would but incline to turn from thee
But a kiss with welcome bland, and touch of thy fair hand
Are all that I'd demand, would'st thou not spurn
For if not mine dear girl
Oh, snowy breasted pearl
May I never from the fair with life return

## 26  Home Boys Home

There appears to be no information available on the origins of this song.
An old English folksong called "The Oak And The Ash" has very similar lyrics in part of the chorus.

Another song very similar in the chorus is called "Home, Dearie, Home" which was used by seamen as a capstan sea shanty and dates back to the early 19th century.

Key: D

When I was a young boy sure I longed to see the world, to
sail a-round the sea in ships and see the sails un-furled. I went to seek my
fortune on the far side of the hill. I have wand-ered far and wide and of the
tra-vel had my fill, *and now it's home, boys, home!*
*Home I'd like to be! Home for a while in the old coun-tr-*
*y, where the oak and the ash and the bon-ny row-an-tree are*
*all a-grow-ing green-er in the old coun-tr-y.*

Well I left my love behind me and I sailed across the tide
I said that I'd be back again and take her for my bride
But many years have passed and gone and still I'm far away
I know she is my fond true-love and waiting for the day
*Chorus*

Now I've learned there's more to life than to wander and to roam
Happiness and peace of mind can best be found at home
For money can't buy happiness and money cannot bind
So I'm going back tomorrow to the girl I left behind
*Chorus*

Glendalough, Wicklow
Oratory, known as 'St. Kevin's Kitchen'

The alter in Kilmainham Gaol at which Joseph Plunkett and Grace Gifford were married hours before his execution
The alter was made by a prisoner, James Lawlor, in the 19th century
The inscription on the back of the alter says, 'James Lawlor,  7 years,  Stealing a wheel off a cart.'

# Joseph Plunkett and Grace Gifford

Joseph Mary Plunkett (1887 - 1916) was a poet, an idealist and a revolutionary. He was born in Dublin, the son of Count George Noble Plunkett, a papal count and curator of the National Museum.

He received his education at Belvedere College in Dublin, Stonyhurst College in Lancashire and at University College Dublin. As an academic he had a keen interest in Irish culture and was a co-founder of the literary journal 'The Irish Review'. He was also a founder member of the Irish Theatre in 1914.

He contracted tuberculosis as a young man and spent time on the Mediterranean coast and in North Africa in order to improve his condition.

Plunkett met another Irish Revolutionary, Thomás McDonagh while he was studying the Irish language for the Dublin University matriculation examinations and the two men struck up an instant friendship, both being interested in Irish culture, poetry and mysticism.

His first book of poems, entitled 'The Circle and the Sword' was published in 1911.

Plunkett took over 'The Irish Review' and became its editor when it ran into financial difficulties. Under his control the journal became more political in its content and supported the Sinn Féin movement and highlighted the plight of the workers during the 1913 Dublin lock-out.

He was a member of the Irish Republican Brotherhood, a covert organisation whose primary aim was the overthrow of British rule in Ireland by forceful means.

In 1915 Plunkett travelled to Germany to assist Sir Roger Casement, an Irish Nationalist, to procure arms and assistance from the German Government for a revolution against Britain in Ireland.

He was appointed to the Council of the Irish Volunteers which was the main force behind the 1916 Rising. He was one of the chief military strategists for the rebellion and was appointed Director of Military Operations for the Rising. The revolution was planned for April 1916 and it began by the taking of the General Post Office in the heart of Dublin on Easter Monday April 24th 1916. The Provisional Government established the GPO as its headquarters and Plunkett was stationed there with a young captain by the name of Michael Collins (see page 18) as his aide-de-camp. He was very ill at the time and was recovering from major surgery on glands in his neck. He was heavily bandaged and took little active part in the rebellion.

The Provisional Government issued a Proclamation establishing independent rule for all the people of Ireland. The document, which was posted up on walls throughout the city carried the signatures of seven members of the Provisional Government. Joseph Plunkett's name was among them, as was that of Thomás McDonagh

Following the surrender of the Provisional Government on April 29th Plunkett was tried by court-martial and executed by firing squad on May 4th, 1916.

On the night before his execution, he was permitted to marry his sweetheart, Grace Gifford. They had originally planned to marry on Easter Sunday.

Grace Gifford (1888 - 1955) lived with her family in the affluent suburb of Rathmines in south Dublin. Her father, Frederick Gifford, was a wealthy Catholic solicitor but her mother, Isabella Burton, was Protestant. In the Gifford household the sons were raised as Catholics and the daughters as Protestants.

In 1904 Grace entered the Dublin Metropolitan School of Art where she studied under the acclaimed artist William Orpen. She soon gained a reputation as a cartoonist with a gifted talent for caricature.

Having spent some time in England studying at the Slade School of Art in London she returned to Ireland and worked as an illustrator and cartoonist, many of her subjects being the politicians and figures of the Irish Literary Revival.

Through mutual acquaintances, the Gifford sisters - Grace, Muriel and Sydney - were introduced to some of the Irish revolutionary leaders, among whom were Thomás McDonagh and Joseph Plunkett. Muriel struck up a relationship with McDonagh (they married later) and Grace became friendly with Plunkett.

Soon the friendship of the young cartoonist and the idealistic revolutionary grew into love and they planned to marry on Easter Sunday 1916. When Plunkett realised that the rebellion against British rule would probably be well under way by Easter Sunday he vowed to her that he would marry her even if he were incarcerated in prison.

Following Plunkett's court-martial and death sentence the authorities agreed to permit the marriage of the lovers in Kilmainham Gaol.

Joseph Plunkett was scheduled to be executed by firing squad at 4am on May 4th. Grace arrived at Kilmainham Gaol on the evening of May 3rd. She was kept waiting until, at 1.30am on May 4th, she was led into the tiny prison chapel and was joined by her sweetheart, weak, handcuffed and under heavy guard.

Owing to a lighting failure the marriage was performed by the Reverend Eugene McCarthy with the aid of a single candle held by a British soldier. They were both twenty-eight years of age. The surrounding walls of the chapel were lined with British soldiers, bayonets fixed. Two British soldiers acted as witnesses.

Immediately after the brief ceremony the couple were separated and Plunkett was returned to his cell. A little later the new bride was permitted to visit her husband in his cell. Fifteen soldiers stood guard in the cell and when the officer announced "Ten minutes are up.", Grace knew that she would never see her beloved again.

Joseph Plunkett was led out to the Stonebreakers Yard at Kilmainham Gaol and shot dead by firing squad.

The previous day, May 3rd, his close companion and future brother-in-law, Thomás McDonagh, had been executed.

Grace Plunkett never married again and died in 1955, forever remembering that fateful morning on May 4th, 1916, when she became the wife of her sweetheart, Joseph Plunkett.

## 30  The Kerry Dances

No information appears to be available in relation to the origins of this song.
It owes its continued popularity to a fine recording of it by the Irish tenor Count John McCormack (1884 - 1945).

Kerry is a county in the south west of Ireland and the County Town is Tralee.
Kerry is renowned for its many tourist attractions, including the towns of Tralee, Killarney, Dingle and Kenmare.

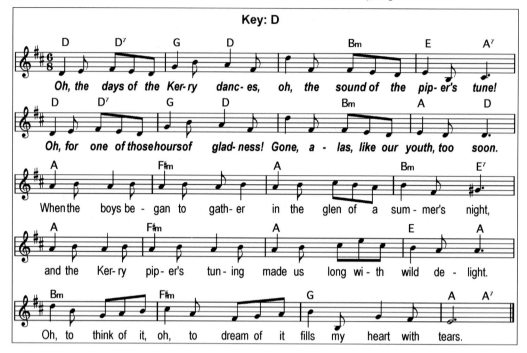

**Key: D**

Oh, the days of the Ker-ry danc-es, oh, the sound of the pip-er's tune!

Oh, for one of those hours of glad-ness! Gone, a - las, like our youth, too soon.

When the boys be - gan to gath-er in the glen of a sum - mer's night,

and the Ker-ry pip-er's tun - ing made us long wi - th wild de - light.

Oh, to think of it, oh, to dream of it fills my heart with tears.

### Chorus

*Was there ever a sweeter colleen in the dance than Eily More
Or a prouder lad than Thady as he boldly took the floor
"Lads and lassies to your places, up the middle and down again!"
And the merry hearted laughter ringing through the happy glen
Oh to think of it! Oh to dream of it!
Fills my heart with tears

### Chorus

*The first two lines are sung to the same melody as the chorus

Open-air set dancing

There appears to be no information available in relation to the origin or composer of this popular ballad.

A 'Peeler' is the slang term for a member of the English police force and is derived from the name of the Home Secretary, Robert Peel, who established the first Metropolitan Police, in 1829.

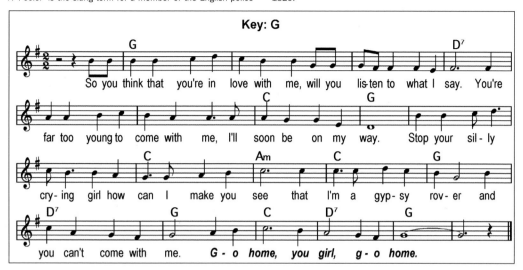

**Key: G**

So you think that you're in love with me, will you lis-ten to what I say. You're far too young to come with me, I'll soon be on my way. Stop your sil - ly cry - ing girl how can I make you see that I'm a gyp- sy rov - er and you can't come with me. *G - o home, you girl, g - o home.*

You met me at the marketplace when your ma was not with you
You liked my long brown ringlets and my handkerchief of blue
Although I'm very fond of you and you asked me home to tea
I am a gypsy rover and you can't come with me
*Chorus*

Your brother is a Peeler and he would put me in jail
If he knew I was a poacher and I hunt your lord's best game
Your daddy is a gentleman, your mammy's just as grand
But I'm a gypsy rover; I'll not be your husband
*Chorus*

The hour is drawing on my love and your ma's expecting thee
Don't you say you met me here for I'm just a gypsy
Please let go my jacket now; your love will have to wait
For I am twenty-two years old and you are only eight
*Chorus*

Lough Owel, Westmeath

## 32 The Bonny Boy

This ballad is also known as "Daily Growing" and "The Bonny Boy Is Young (But Growing)" and "The Trees They Grow So High". It first appeared in James Johnson's "The Scots Musical Museum" in 1792 under the title of "Lady Mary Ann" but it could be a lot older, as child marriages were common in the Middle Ages. There is speculation that the ballad may be based on the marriage in 1631 between the young Laird of Craighton to Elizabeth Innes, a girl several years older. He died three years after the marriage.

There are various different arrangements of this old folksong, including one by the famous English composer, Benjamin Britten.

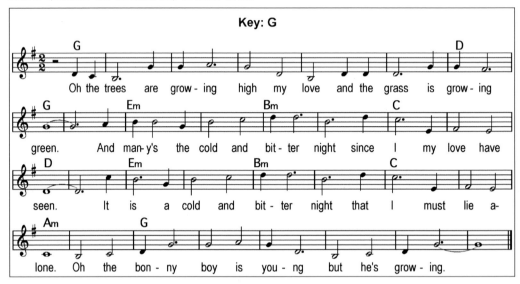

Oh Father dear father I think you did me wrong
For to go and get me married to one who is so young
For he is only sixteen years and I am twenty-one
And the bonny boy is young and still growing

Oh daughter dear daughter I did not do you wrong
For to go and get you married to one who is so young
I know he'll be a match for you when I am dead and gone
Oh the bonny boy is young but he's growing

Oh Father dear father I'll tell you what I'll do
I'll send my love to college for another year or two
And all around his college cap I'll tie a ribbon blue
Just to show the other girls that he's married

At evening when strolling down by the college wall
You'd see the young collegiates a-playing at the ball
You'd see him in amongst them there, the fairest of them all
He's my bonny boy, he's young but he's growing

At the early age of sixteen years he was a married man
And at the age of seventeen the father of a son
But at the age of eighteen o'er his grave the grass grew strong
Cruel death put an end to his growing

I will make my love a shroud of the highest Holland brown
And whilst I am a-weaving it my tears they will flow down
For once I had a true love but now he's lying low
And I'll nurse his bonny boy while he's growing

Misty afternoon, Killarney National Park, Kerry

Mobile phones and thatched cottages!
Taking a break from repairing a thatched roof
Bunratty Folk Park, Clare

This song is also known as "The Ploughboy" and it first appeared in the book "Traditional Tunes", a collection of folksongs published in 1891 and compiled by the English folksong collector and music scholar, Frank Kidson.

The lark (or to use its official name 'Skylark', or alauda arvensis) is a very common bird in Ireland. It is estimated that over one million skylarks breed in Ireland each year. Their favourite habitats are the open country and coastal dunes. They make their nests on the ground, usually under clumps of tall grass. They often perch and sing on fence posts.

One of the great characteristics of skylarks is their practice of flying at high altitude especially over stubble fields where they find most of their food - cereal grain and insects.

The lark is one of the first birds to be heard in the morning in open countryside - hence they have become symbolic of the morning and the dawn of a new day. Its continuous song consists of a constant jumble of twittering, chirping and warbling sounds, often including the imitation of other song birds. It sings as it ascends into the heavens and hovers on fluttering wings, sometimes until it is almost out of sight.

There is another song in this book relating to the skylark. See "My Singing Bird" - page 20

The lark in the morn - ing she ris - es off her nest and she flies up to the heav - ens with the dew all on her breast. Like the jol - ly plough - boy she whist - les and she sings and she comes home in the eve - nings with the dew all on her wings.

Oh Roger the ploughboy he is a dashing blade
He goes whistling and singing in yonder leafy shade
He met with dark-eyed Susan; she's handsome I declare
And she is far more enticing than the birds all in the air

As they were coming home from the rakes of the town
The meadow being all mown and the grass had been cut down
And as they should chance to tumble all in the new-mown hay
"Oh, it's kiss me now or never" this bonnie lass would say

When twenty long weeks were over and had passed
Her mammy asked the reason why she thickened 'round the waist
"It was the pretty ploughboy" this lassie then did say
"For he asked me for to tumble all in the new-mown hay"

Here's a health to you ploughboys wherever you may be
That like to have a bonnie lass a-sitting on each knee
With a pint of good strong porter he'll whistle and he'll sing
And the ploughboy is as happy as a prince or as a king

# Bunclody

Bunclody is a town situated in County Wexford, on Ireland's east coast, about 76 miles from Dublin. At Bunclody the River Slaney joins with the River Clody. To the south-west rises Mount Leinster (2610 feet).

The town was formerly known as Newtownbarry in recognition of its patron James Barry, Sovereign of Naas, whose daughter

Judith married John Maxwell who was granted a patent for Fairs at Bunclody in 1720.

During the 1798 Rebellion insurgents under Father Kearns attacked Bunclody in an unsuccessful attempt to open communications with their comrades in Carlow and Wicklow.

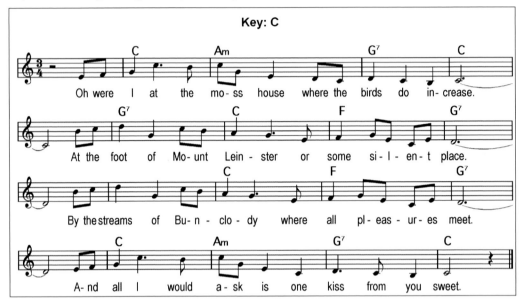

The streams of Bunclody they flow down so free
By the streams of Bunclody I'm longing to be
A-drinking strong liquor in the height of my cheer
Here's a health to Bunclody and the lass I love dear

Oh, 'tis why my love slights me as you might understand
For she has a freehold and I have no land
She has great stores of riches and a fine sum of gold
And everything fitting a house to uphold

If I were a clerk and could write a good hand
I would write my love a letter that she would understand
For I am a young fellow that is wounded in love
Once I lived in Bunclody but now must remove

So fare thee well father and mother, adieu
My sisters and brothers farewell unto you
I am bound for Americay my fortune to try
When I think of Bunclody I'm ready to die

Peaceful morning scene on the road between Gorey and Bunclody

# Nora

This song is also known as "Maggie" and was included by Sean O'Casey (with additional lyrics by himself) in his play "The Plough and the Stars".

The original "Maggie" was written by the Canadian, George Johnson in 1863 to a melody composed by James A. Butterfield.

**Key: D**

The vio - lets were scent - ing the woods No- ra, dis - play - ing their charms to the bees, when I first said I loved on - ly you, Nora, and you said you loved on - ly me. The chest - nut's bloom beams through the glade, No- ra, the ro - bin sang from ev - ery tree. When I first said I loved on- ly you, No - ra, and you said you loved on - ly me.

The golden dewed daffodils shone, Nora
And danced in the breeze on the lea
When I first said I loved only you, Nora
And you said you loved only me
The birds in the trees sang their songs, Nora
Of happier transports to be
When I first said I loved only you, Nora
And you said you loved only me

Our hopes they have never come true, Nora
Our dreams they were never to be
Since I first said I loved only you, Nora
And you said you loved only me
The violets are withered and gone, Nora
I cry for the years as they flee
Since I first said I loved only you Nora
And you said you loved only me

Roadside scene, Limerick

This song is included in the collection "Irish Country Songs" (1909) edited by the collector, Herbert Hughes, where he states that it is an old song which originated in County Antrim (Northern Ireland).

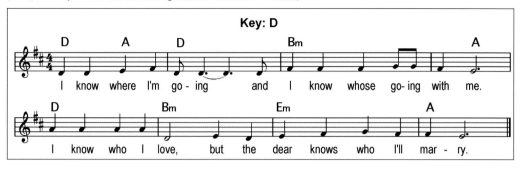

I know where I'm go-ing and I know whose go-ing with me.
I know who I love, but the dear knows who I'll mar - ry.

Some will say he's dark, some will say he's bonny
But the fairest of them all is my handsome noble Johnny

I have stockings of silk, shoes of fine green leather
Combs to bind my hair and a ring for every finger

Feather beds are soft and painted rooms are bonny
But I would leave them all to be with my darling Johnny

*(Repeat first verse)*

Keel Beach, Achill Island

Ben Bulben, Sligo

# Diarmuid and Gráinne

*In the pre-Norman era - prior to the 12th century - Ireland had been ruled by High Kings, and their centre of administration was at Tara in County Meath.*

*One of the High Kings of Ireland was Cormac MacArt. During his reign he appointed Fionn MacCumhaill as the Chieftan of the Fianna, a band of warriors who gave allegiance to the king but still maintained their independence.*

*Tensions arose between Fionn and Cormac and Fionn was anxious to heal the rift, so he asked for Cormac's daughter's hand in marriage. Her name was Gráinne and she was very beautiful.*

*Fionn was quite old but notwithstanding this, Cormac agreed to the match. He, too, was anxious to dampen the tensions between Fionn and himself and he felt that making Fionn his son-in-law would alleviate the problem and gain him a powerful ally at the same time. Nobody, of course, had any consideration for what Gráinne felt about the arrangement.*

*A magnificent banquet was held at Tara to celebrate the betrothal and chieftans and noblemen travelled from the four corners of Ireland to attend.*

*Gráinne, however, was determined that she would not become the wife of an old man and she maintained a silence at the feast until she caught sight of the young Diarmuid Ua Duibhne among the guests. She instantly fell in love with him and couldn't take her eyes off him for the rest of the evening.*

*She concocted a plan which would free her from her present predicament. She prepared a magic potion which she served to all the guests except Diarmuid and some of his closest companions. The potion caused all the guests who had drunk it to fall into a deep sleep.*

*When the potion had taken its affect Gráinne approached Diarmuid, told him that she was in love with him and asked him to take her far away from Tara and Fionn.*

*Diarmuid, who was also in love with Gráinne, refused her request out of loyalty to Cormac, his king, and Fionn, his chieftan. However, undaunted, she put a 'geis' on him - an enchanted spell which compelled him to do as she asked. The young lovers thus fled the castle at the dead of night and embarked on a seven year journey of flight which became widely known as "The Pursuit of Diarmuid and Gráinne"*

*As they tirelessly journeyed from hideout to hideout throughout the length and breadth of the country they were pursued relentlessly by the tenacious and enraged Fionn, and the Fianna.*

*On several occasions they were nearly caught, the hounds of Fionn being on their heels, but the couple, driven on by their love for each other, evaded capture each time.*

*They eventually arrived at an impenetrable glen called Kesh Corran in Sligo. Feeling that they were safe in the seclusion of the place, they set up home there.*

*For many years they lived a happy and normal life at Kesh Corran, and Gráinne bore Diarmuid four healthy sons.*

*The love Diarmuid and Gráinne felt for each other never weakened and they were peacefully and happily growing old together. However, one day Gráinne, who missed her extended family, suggested to Diarmuid that he make amends with Fionn, who at this stage had given up the pursuit. Diarmuid, who also missed his former friends and comrades, happily acceded to the suggestion and he invited Fionn to Kesh Corran.*

*Fionn accepted the invitation and stayed for many months as a guest of the lovers. However, Fionn discovered that his jealousy and antagonism towards Diarmuid had been rekindled by observing the devoted couple together. He wanted to challenge Diarmuid to a fight but he knew that custom prevented him from fighting his host directly. He therefore devised a clever plan.*

*Fionn was aware that a 'geis' had been put on Diarmuid as a young boy never to fight a wild boar. If he did, he would be killed by the beast. It was for this reason that he never hunted wild boar, which were plentiful on the nearby Ben Bulben.*

*One night Fionn tricked Diarmuid into joining a hunting expedition to Ben Bulben. Gráinne, who was aware of the 'geis' on Diarmuid tried desperately to dissuade him but she was left in despair as he departed with Fionn and the Fianna, bound for Ben Bulben.*

*When they reached the plateau of Ben Bulben Fionn managed to steal away and leave Diarmuid on his own. It wasn't long before Diarmuid was confronted by a fierce wild boar which immediately attacked him.*

*Diarmuid and his trusty hound fought savagely with the boar until Diarmuid eventually killed him. However Diarmuid had been badly gored in the struggle.*

*Diarmuid knew that the curse of the 'geis' was upon him and that he was dying. But he also knew that Fionn held the power of healing with water. When Fionn arrived back to Ben Bulben Diarmuid asked him to use his powers to heal him.*

*On two occasions Fionn collected water in his hands from the nearby stream but purposely let it slip through his fingers as he returned to Diarmuid. However he began to feel remorse when he remembered all the past heroic deeds of Diarmuid and rushed to the stream to collect more water to save him. When he returned to Diarmuid with the water safely held in his cupped hands, Diarmuid was dead.*

*Gráinne was stricken with grief at the news of Diarmuid's death. However over a long age the mists of Time gradually clouded Gráinne's rage against Fionn and she eventually married him and lived out her days in a place called Allmu in County Kildare.*

**Twenty-One Years**

Dartmoor Prison is located in Princetown in the English county of Devon.

It was built in 1809 to house prisoners of war but was converted into a civilian prison in 1851.

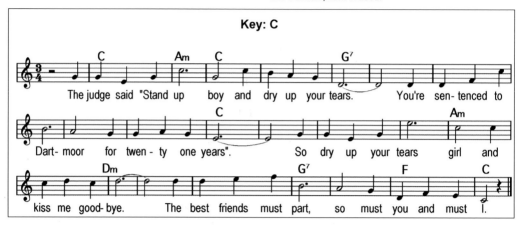

**Key: C**

The judge said "Stand up boy and dry up your tears. You're sen- tenced to Dart- moor for twen- ty one years". So dry up your tears girl and kiss me good- bye. The best friends must part, so must you and must I.

I hear the train coming, 'twill be here at nine
To take me to Dartmoor to serve out my time
I look down the railway and plainly I see
You standing there waiving your goodbyes to me

Six months have gone by, love, I wish I were dead
This cold dreary jail and a stone for my head
It's raining, it's hailing, the moon shows no light
Why won't you tell me, love, why you never write?

I've counted the days, love, I've counted the nights
I've counted the footsteps, I've counted the lights
I've counted the raindrops, I've counted the stars
I've counted a million of these prison bars

I've waited, I've trusted, I've longed for the day
A lifetime so lonely; my hair's turning grey
My thoughts are for you, love, till I'm out of my mind
For twenty-one years is a mighty long time

Tarbert Jail, Kerry

*(Verses and chorus have the same melody)*

This ballad is probably of English origin and is also known as "The Bold Grenadier". The words and sentiments are also very similar to several verses of a ballad which was printed in 1675 by W. Olney of London entitled "The Nightingale's Song: Or The Soldier's Rare Musick, And The Maid's Recreation" to be found in the Bodleian Library in Oxford University. The broadside says that it is to be sung to the melody of "No, No, Not I".

There is also another very popular and quite different English ballad called "The Nightingale" which begins with the line 'My love he was a rich farmer's son'.

The romantic nightingale is a long distance migrant cousin of the familiar garden Robin. It is only active on these islands for a few weeks in late Spring. The most unique feature of this bird is, of course, that it sings at night-time and has therefore gained a reputation as a bird of romance. Its chirp or voice is very varied and noted for its contralto qualities with whistles and haunting repeated phrases.

We Irish would have quite an affiliation to the nightingale. You mightn't see us very much during the day but at night-time we can be heard singing over long distances! There is one subtle difference between ourselves and these beautiful birds, however - we tend to consume lots of beer in the course of our singing (indeed very often that is the principal reason for our singing in the first place). I don't think that the nightingale partakes of that activity!

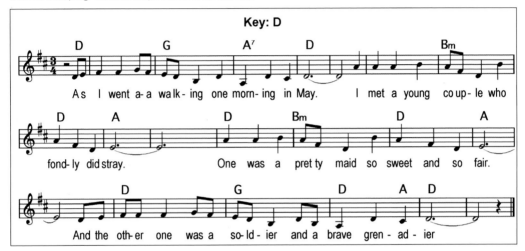

*And they kissed so sweet and comforting as they clung to each other*
*They went arm-in-arm along the road like sister and brother*
*They went arm-in-arm along the road till they came to a stream*
*And they both sat down together for to hear the nightingale sing*

From out of his knapsack he took a fine fiddle
And he played her such a merry tune with a hi-diddle-diddle
And he played her such a merry tune that the trees they did ring
And they both sat down together for to hear the nightingale sing
*Chorus*

Oh soldier, handsome soldier will you marry me
Oh no said the soldier that never can be
For I have a wife at home in my own country
And she is the sweetest little flower that you ever did see
*Chorus*

Now I am off to India for seven long years
Drinking wine and strong whiskey instead of cold beers
And if ever I return again it will be in the spring
And we'll both sit down together for to hear the nightingale sing
*Chorus*

**Sliabh Gallion Brae**

This is a mournful song of exile and emigration centred in the area of Sliabh Gallion.
A brae is a slope or hillside.
Sliabh Gallion is one of the mountain peaks of the Sperrin Mountains which occupy parts of Counties Derry and Tyrone in the Province of Ulster in the north of Ireland.
A beautiful version of the song is to be found on the album "Winter's Crossing" (1998) by James Galway and Phil Coulter. It was also recorded by The Clancy Brothers and Tommy Makem.

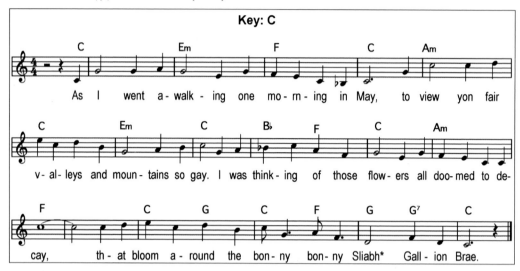

Key: C

As I went a-walk-ing one mo-rn-ing in May, to view yon fair v-al-leys and moun-tains so gay. I was think-ing of those flow-ers all doo-med to de-cay, th-at bloom a-round the bon-ny bon-ny Sliabh* Gall-ion Brae.

How oft in the morning with my dog and my gun
I roamed through the glens for joy and for fun
But those days are all over and I must go away
So farewell unto ye bonny bonny Sliabh Gallion Brae

How oft in the evening with the sun in the west
I roved hand in hand with the one I love the best
But the hopes of youth are vanished and now I'm far away
So farewell unto ye bonny bonny Sliabh Gallion Brae

It was not for the want of employment at home
That caused us poor exiles in sorrow to roam
But those tyrannising landlords they would not let us stay
So farewell unto ye bonny bonny Sliabh Gallion Brae

* Pronounced "shleeve" (mountain)

# The Banks Of The Roses

This ballad dates from the end of the 18th century and is thought to have originated in County Limerick. It's also known by the title "The Banks Of The Red Roses"

There are many versions of this ballad to be found and in some of them Johnny takes his lover to a cave and murders her, burying her body on the Banks of the Roses.

This song is not related in any way to the popular English ballad "The Banks Of The Sweet Primroses".

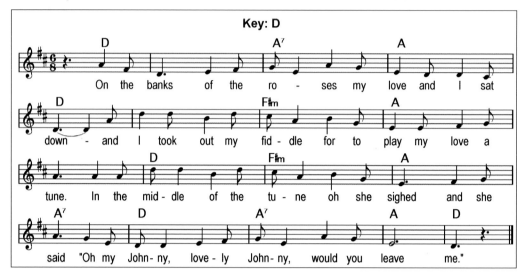

**Key: D**

On the banks of the ro - ses my love and I sat down - and I took out my fid - dle for to play my love a tune. In the mid - dle of the tu - ne oh she sighed and she said "Oh my John- ny, love - ly John- ny, would you leave me."

"When I was just a young girl I heard my father say
'I'd sooner see you dead, my girl, and buried in the clay
Rather than be married to a roving runaway
On the lovely sweet banks of the roses' ".

Oh well now I am a runaway and sure I'll let you know
That I can take a bottle and drink with anyone
If her father doesn't like me he can keep his daughter home
Then young Johnny will go roving with another

If I ever get wedded 'twill be in the month of May
When the leaves they are green and the meadows they are gay
And me and my true love will sit and sport and play
By the lovely sweet banks of the roses

View from The Vee Gap, Tipperary

*(Verses and chorus have the same melody)*

This ballad, full of innuendo and double-meaning, is a derivative of an old English ballad called "The German Musicianer" in which the gentleman in question tuned the woman's piano as opposed to winding her clock. It doesn't really matter - it all came down to the same thing in the end!

There is a Grosvenor Square situated in Dublin city, but I doubt if that's the intended location referred to in the song.

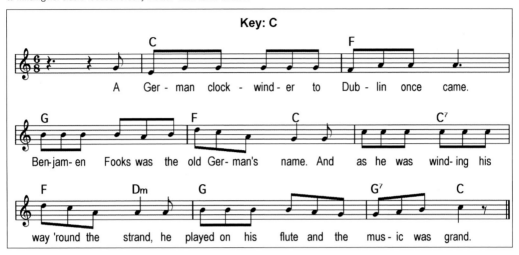

With me toor-a-lumma-lumma, toor-a-lumma-lumma, toor-a-lie-ay
*Toor-a-lie, oor-a-lie, orr-a-lie-ay*
*Toor-a-lumma-lumma, toor-a-lumma-lumma, toor-a-lie-ay*
*Toor-a-lie, oor-a-lie, orr-a-lie-ay*

Now there was a young lady from Grosvenor Square
Who said that her clock was in need of repair
In walks the bold German and to her delight
In less than five minutes he had her put right
*Chorus*

Now as they were seated down on the floor
There started a very loud knock on the door
In walked her husband and great was his shock
To see the bold German wind up his wife's clock
*Chorus*

The husband says he "Oh wife, Mary Ann
Don't let that bold German come in here again
He wound up your clock and left mine on the shelf
If your oul' clock needs winding I'll wind it myself!"
*Chorus*

Martin McGreal outside his butcher shop, Achill Island

This is a popular ballad, sung extensively in Ireland.
It's origins are unknown and the place name used in the first
verse changes depending on the location of the singer, or the

venue where it's being performed!
The song is included in Paul Brewster's book "Ballads and Songs
of Indiana" (1940)

Key: D

In Dublin Town where I did dwell, A butcher boy
I loved so well. He courted me by night and day.
He stole from me my heart a - way.

I wish my baby it was born, and smiling on its daddy's knee
And my poor body to be dead and gone, with the long green grass growing over me

I'll go upstairs and make my bed; "What's there to do?" my mother said
My mother she has followed me, and saying "what's to come of thee?"
*Chorus*

"Oh mother dear you little know, my pain and sorrow and my woe
Go get a chair and sit me down; with pen and ink I'll write it down"

Her father he came home that night, enquiring for his heart's delight
He went upstairs the door he broke, and found her hanging by a rope
*Chorus*

He took a knife and cut her down, and in her bosom these lines he found
"Oh what a foolish girl was I, to give my heart to a butcher boy"

"Go dig my grave both wide and deep; put a marble stone at my head and feet
And in the middle a turtle dove, so the world might know I died for love
*Chorus*

# Robert Emmet and Sarah Curran

*R*obert Emmet (1778 - 1803) is regarded as one of the most romantic and influential of Ireland's many revolutionaries and is still, to this day, a national hero. Emmet was born in Dublin into financially comfortable circumstances. His father was the surgeon to the Lord Lieutenant in Ireland.

He was educated at Trinity College Dublin, where he was renowned for his skills in oratory and won many accolades in the College Historical Society. He was expelled from the university for his radical nationalist activities and for his support of the revolutionary Society of United Irishmen, of which he was a member. In 1800 he visited France in the hope of gaining their support for a rebellion against British rule in Ireland. However he quickly became disillusioned with the attitudes of the French and felt that if the Irish won freedom with the help of the French they would find themselves merely changing from British oppression to French oppression.

He decided therefore that if the Irish people wished to gain freedom they would need to take the necessary action themselves. He returned to Ireland and along with a group of other revolutionary nationalists prepared the ground for a new rebellion to win Irish freedom.

Using his wealth he began to purchase facilities and rent premises in Dublin to manufacture weapons and explosives. He designed an innovative pike which could be concealed under a cloak, being fitted with a special hinge.

By 1803 Emmet was the leader of the group of nationalists organising the rebellion. Preparations for the rebellion were being successfully concealed by Emmet and his followers until a premature explosion in one of his depots on 16th July 1803, killing one of his followers, forced him to bring the plans for the rebellion forward.

In spite of the fact that he was relying heavily on the support of seasoned veterans from the 1798 rebellion and that this support filtered away, the rebellion went ahead in Dublin on the evening of July 23rd, 1803.

Emmet, leading a motley band of drunkards, casual onlookers and some dedicated but inexperienced nationalists, attempted an attack on Dublin Castle which was a complete failure. British troops managed to quell the 'disturbance' in a matter of hours.

Emmet fled into the Dublin mountains but moved his hiding place to Harolds Cross in the outskirts of Dublin in order to be near to his sweetheart, Sarah Curran. He was captured by the British authorities at a house in Harolds Cross on August 25th 1803. After the sentence of death had been passed on him he delivered an address to the court which is considered to be the finest 'speech from the dock' of any condemned revolutionary in Irish history, ending with the famous words -

"Let no man write my epitaph; for as no man who knows my motives dare now vindicate them, let not prejudice or ignorance asperse them. Let them and me rest in obscurity and peace and my tomb remain uninscribed and my memory in oblivion until other times and other men can do justice to my character. When my country takes her place among the nations of the earth, then and only then, let my epitaph be written. I have done"

On September 19th, Emmet was found guilty of high treason and he was executed on the following day outside the gates of St. Catherine's Church on Thomas Street.

Robert Emmet remains an idol in many Irish minds. His deeds and exploits, in such a short life, are discussed and analysed, his memory is revered in folk-ballads, and sketches and portraits of him are to be found in countless homes and public buildings throughout Ireland and farther afield.

Yet his insurrection in 1803 was a complete failure, he left no significant political writings and nobody knows what he really looked like.

Robert Emmet became the idol and symbol for a nation, and a romantic legend, due to a combination of factors - an idealistic, wealthy, educated young man cut down for his principles, the brilliance of his speech from the dock at his trial, the innocence and naivete in his military plans, his lost grave, and, of course, his passionate and clandestine love affair with his sweetheart, Sarah Curran.

Sarah Curran (1782 - 1808) was born in County Cork,

the daughter of John Philpot Curran, a successful lawyer and politician.

She was raised in Rathfarnham at the foothills of the Dublin Mountains. Her childhood was unhappy and she described painfully her melancholy home and confined circumstances.

Her parents' marriage broke up in a very acrimonious and public manner which contributed to her woes.

She was sent to Waterford where she began to develop into a talented musician, as a pianist and harpist She also had a fine singing voice. She had a deep faith and spent long hours reading and studying the bible.

Sarah made her social debut at a ball in County Wicklow in 1799. She was developing into a considerable beauty and made a lasting impression on the assembled guests, one of whom was the young Robert Emmet.

Emmet, who was a friend of Sarah's brother, Richard, used every excuse he could to spend time with Richard at the Curran home in Rathfarnham so that he could be near Sarah. Emmet became increasingly enchanted by this beautiful, charming and witty girl and a close friendship began between the two of them. This friendship soon developed into romance and soon they were both deeply in love with each other.

This relationship was carried on in secret for fear that Sarah's father might learn of it and disapprove of the young revolutionary. Even Emmet's close friend Richard wasn't aware of it until after the 1803 rebellion.

Although on the run after the failed rebellion, Emmet chose to stay in Harolds Cross, a few short miles from Rathfarnham, so that he could be near to Sarah. Emmet was staying in a lodging house under an assumed name and the lovers corresponded regularly by letter. These letters show that, in spite of the awful and dangerous predicament he found himself in, his beloved Sarah was predominant in his mind. In her letters to him Sarah admitted that she longed to see him again but also accepted that he should take no risks in that regard. Although Sarah was aware of Emmet's plans for a revolution she had never breathed a word of them to

anyone. During cross-examination Emmet lied to protect his beloved from prosecution.

As no one knew of their relationship it was days before Sarah learned of Emmet's arrest. However, in spite of her appeals for him to destroy her letters, Emmet had foolishly kept some of them and these were found on him when he was arrested. Although these letters were unsigned Emmet was tricked into revealing her identity. Horrified at the prospect of her being placed under arrest or ill-treated Emmet was prepared to offer any deal to the authorities to ensure her protection. He was prepared to remain silent at his trial if the authorities would leave Sarah alone. The authorities refused to negotiate and it is interesting to speculate as to how Emmet would have been regarded had he not made his famous and impassioned speech from the dock.

The authorities raided and searched the Curran home in Rathfarnham and John Philpot Curran was enraged to learn of his daughter's clandestine affair with Emmet. His main concern appeared to be the potential damage to his own reputation.

On the morning of his execution Emmet wrote one final letter to his sweetheart, expressing his deep love for her and regretting that events had turned out the way they had.

After Emmet's execution Sarah was banished to County Cork by her father. Far away from the turmoil of Dublin and the memories of her beloved Emmet she slowly began to recover her strength. However she suffered from bouts of depression and was prone to wild tantrums.

In 1805 she accepted the proposal of marriage from Captain R. Henry Sturgeon, a talented engineer in the British army. Sturgeon was a kind and loving husband and her marriage fluctuated between periods of immense joy and others of great depression.

She never really recovered from the loss of her sweetheart, the young, romantic and idealistic Robert Emmet.

In May 1808 she died at Kent, having surrendered to illnesses both physical and mental. She was buried in the town where she was born - Newmarket in County Cork.

St. Catherine's Church, Dublin. Scene of Robert Emmet's execution

51

**Easy And Slow**

The Irish Playwright Sean O'Casey (1880 - 1964) included this ballad in his play "Red Roses For Me", although it is unclear as to whether or not he composed the song himself.
"Red Roses For Me" was written in 1943 and was first performed in the Olympia Theatre, Dublin the same year.
Christchurch, Thomas Street and Kingsbridge are all located in Dublin's south inner city. The Park referred to is Phoenix Park
Dungannon is a town in County Tyrone, Northern Ireland
The song was recorded by The Clancy Brothers for their album "Flowers of the Valley" (1970).
It was also recorded by other legendary Irish balladeers Jim McCann and the late, great Ronnie Drew of The Dubliners.

All along Thomas Street, down to the Liffey, the sunshine was gone and the evening grew dark
Along by Kingsbridge and begod in a jiffy, me arms were around her beyond in the Park
*Chorus*

From city or county the girl she's a jewel, and well made for gripping the most of them are
But any young man he is really a fool, if he tries at the first time to go a bit far
*Chorus*

If you should go to the town of Dungannon, you'll search till your eyes they are weary or blind
Be you lying or walking or sitting or running, a lassie like Annie you never will find
*Chorus*

# Believe Me If All Those Endearing Young Charms 53

This song was written in 1808 by Thomas Moore (1779 - 1852). It is believed that Moore wrote it for a woman (perhaps his wife) who had suffered facial scars due to an attack of smallpox. The lyrics were set to an Irish air from the early 1800's. For further details about Thomas Moore and his songs see the Additional Notes at the front of this book.

It is not while beauty and truth are thine own
And thy cheeks unprofaned by a tear
That the fervour and faith of a soul can be known
To which time will but make thee more dear
No, the heart that has truly loved never forgets
But as truly loves on to the close
As the sun-flower turns on her God when he sets
The same look which she turned when he rose

Birthplace of Thomas Moore, Aungier Street, Dublin

The shoreline at Doneen, looking across to the west coast of Clare

Doneen Point is situated on the west coast of Ireland between the towns of Ballybunion and Ballylongford (County Kerry) on the estuary of the River Shannon with fine views across to County Clare.

Kilrush and Kilkee are two small towns on the west coast of Clare. On the western shores of County Clare is the wonderfully varied Atlantic coastline with mighty cliffs, caverns and sandy bays. To the north the rugged coast rises 700 feet above the sea at the sheer Cliffs of Moher. Extending for over five miles these cliffs are home to puffins and guillemots, cormorants and rare fossils. My favourite version of this ballad is by the Irish folk singer Christy Moore on his album "Prosperous" recorded in 1971.

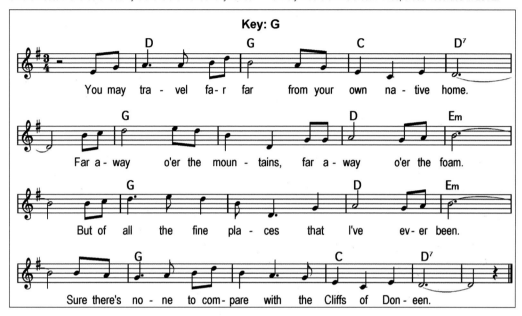

It's a nice place to be on a fine summer's day
Watching all the wild flowers that ne'er do decay
Oh the hares and the pheasants are plain to be seen
Making homes for their young 'round the Cliffs of Doneen

Take a view o'er the mountains, fine sights you'll see there
You'll see the high rocky mountains o'er the west coast of Clare
Oh the towns of Kilkee and Kilrush can be seen
From the high rocky slopes 'round the Cliffs of Doneen

Fare thee well to Doneen, fare thee well for a while
And to all the kind people I'm leaving behind
To the streams and the meadows where late I have been
And the high rocky slopes 'round the Cliffs of Doneen

Fare thee well to Doneen, fare thee well for a while
And although we are parted by the raging sea wild
Once again I will walk with my Irish colleen
'Round the high rocky slopes of the Cliffs of Doneen

# The Good Ship Kangaroo

*(Verses and chorus have the same melody)*

This capstan shanty song, also known as "On board the Kangaroo", is sung in Liverpool and is well-known in Ireland. There are many different versions of the song to be found. Notes from the Grieg-Duncan Folksong Collection suggest that it was composed by Harry Clifton, a music-hall performer and prolific songwriter, and published in 1856.

There were several ships names Kangaroo - a schooner built in Douglas in 1867 and others from Halifax, Nova Scotia and St. John's in Newfoundland. However, there is also a likelihood that the name refers to a fictitious vessel.

Stan Hugill, in his book, "Shanties From The Seven Seas"

considers the tune to be definitely Irish. Seamus Ennis, the legendary Irish piper and collector of folk music for the BBC, collected it from Mrs. Elizabeth Cronin of Macroom in County Cork. Hugill says in his book that it was customary for sailors to buy their wives a washing tub so that they could earn an income while they were at sea.

Burl Ives recorded the song for his album "Songs of Ireland" (1958). The hugely popular Irish group Planxty included it on their 1979 album, "After The Break", resulting in a renewed interest in the song throughout Ireland.

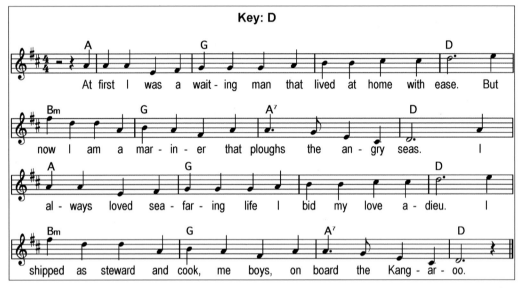

**Key: D**

At first I was a wait-ing man that lived at home with ease. But now I am a mar-in-er that ploughs the an-gry seas. I al-ways loved sea-far-ing life I bid my love a-dieu. I shipped as steward and cook, me boys, on board the Kang-ar-oo.

*Oh I never thought she would prove false or either prove untrue*
*As I sailed away through Milford Bay on board the Kangaroo*

My love she's not a foolish girl her age it is two score
My love she's not a spinster, she's been married twice before
I cannot say it was her wealth that stole my heart away
She was working in the laundry for one and nine a day

"Oh think of me, oh think of me" she mournfully did say
"When you are in a foreign land and I am far away
Now take this lucky thrupenny bit, it'll make you bear in mind
The loving trusting faithful heart you left in tears behind
*Chorus*

"Cheer up, cheer up my own dear love, don't weep so bitterly"
She sobbed, she sighed, she choked, she cried and could not say goodbye
"I won't be gone for very long, 'tis but a month or two
And when I do return again of course I'll marry you"

Our vessel she was homeward bound from many's a far-off shore
And many's the foreign gifts and things unto my love I bore
I brought tortoises from Tenerife and toys from Timbuktu
A China rat, a Bengal cat and a Bombay cockatoo
**Chorus**

Paid off, I sought her dwelling on the street above the town
Where a wiley dame upon the line was hanging out her gown
"Where is my love?". "She's married sir, about six months ago
To a smart young man who drives the van for Chaplin, Son and Co."

Here's health to dreams of married life, to soap, to suds and blue
Heart's true love and patent starch and washing soda too
I'll go unto some distant shore no longer can I stay
And with some China Hottentot I throw myself away
**Chorus**

Fire station, Glencolumbkille, Donegal

# The Meeting Of The Waters

This ballad was written by Thomas Moore (1779 - 1852), one of Ireland's greatest songwriters.

The air is an ancient Irish air "The Old Head of Denis" which is noted in George Petrie's "Ancient Music Of Ireland" (1855) in a slightly different version. Petrie says in the book that he collected this melody from the singing of Biddy Monaghan in Rathcarrick, County Sligo, in 1837.

Written in 1807 this ballad is about a village and vale in County Wicklow, south of Dublin on the easy coast, called Avoca, and the meeting of two rivers, the Avonmore and the Avonbeg. There are two meetings of these rivers in this vicinity - one at a place called

Castle Howard and the other at Woodenbridge. Moore settled the question as to which of the scenes inspired his song in a letter to Lord John Russell in which he wrote "I believe the scene under Castle Howard was the one which suggested the song to me".

Below the Meeting Bridge is the stump of a tree known locally as 'Moore's tree' against which Moore is said to have often rested, contemplating the scene before him.

For further details about Thomas Moore and his songs see the Additional Notes at the front of this book.

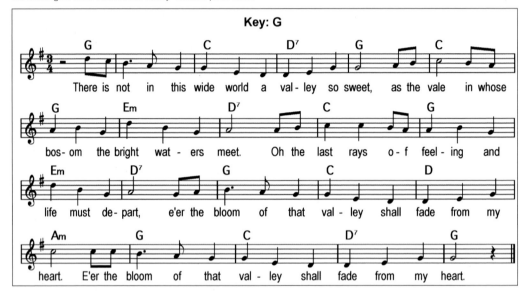

Key: G

There is not in this wide world a val-ley so sweet, as the vale in whose bos-om the bright wat-ers meet. Oh the last rays o-f feel-ing and life must de-part, e'er the bloom of that val-ley shall fade from my heart. E'er the bloom of that val-ley shall fade from my heart.

Yet it was not that Nature had shed o'er the scene
Her purest of crystal and brightest of green
'Twas not her soft magic of streamlet or hill
Oh no! It was something more exquisite still
Oh no! It was something more exquisite still

'Twas that friends, the belov'd of my bosom were near
Who made every dear scene of enchantment more dear
And who felt how the best charms of Nature improve
When we see them reflected from looks that we love
When we see them reflected from looks that we love

Sweet vale of Avoca how calm could I rest
In thy bosom of shade with the friends I love best
Where the storms that we feel in this cold world should cease
And our hearts like thy waters be mingled in peace
And our hearts like thy waters be mingled in peace

Meeting of the Waters, Castle Howard, Wicklow

# The Boys From The County Armagh

This is the county anthem of all folk from County Armagh.

This ballad is attributed to Thomas P. Keenan who also wrote another well-known Irish ballad, "The Old Rustic Bridge By The Mill".

The county of Armagh is situated in the north east of Ireland. It is the smallest of the six counties of Northern Ireland.

The town of Armagh is the ecclesiastical capital of Ireland, the seat both of the Cardinal Archbishop and Catholic Primate of All Ireland, and the Protestant Archbishop. Hence the reference to "cathedral city".

The sacred Book of Armagh, one of Ireland's most precious heirlooms, can be seen in the Library of Trinity College Dublin.

The book is a copy of the New Testament made for Abbot Torbach of Armagh in 807 by the master-scribe Ferdomnach. The book is of special interest to historians because it contains at the front a collection of 7th century texts about Saint Patrick and at the back a copy of the 4th century Life of Saint Martin of Tours.

Newtown, Forkhill, Crossmaglen and Blackwater are well known placenames and towns in County Armagh.

If you're in County Armagh and want to be 'flavour of the month' with the locals, you should have this song well rehearsed as you'll get plenty of opportunities to sing it!

I've travelled that part of the county
Through Newtown, Forkhill, Crossmaglen
Around by the gap of Mount Norris
And home by Blackwater again
Where girls are so fair and so pretty
None better you'll find near or far
But where are the boys that can court them
Like the boys from the County Armagh
**Chorus**

Sligo Town

# Charles Stewart Parnell and Kitty O'Shea

*C*harles Stewart Parnell (1846 - 1891) was a nationalist statesman who believed that the only way to achieve freedom from British rule in Ireland was by parliamentary negotiation and non-violent political agitation. At the height of his popularity he was often referred to as the 'uncrowned king of Ireland'.

He was born into a Protestant landlord family in Avondale, County Wicklow.

Parnell's parents separated when he was six and he spent an unhappy youth. His father died in 1859 and Parnell inherited the Avondale estate.

After an undistinguished spell at Magdalene College Cambridge he returned to Ireland and settled down into a comfortable life as a member of the Wicklow gentry.

In 1874 he became High Sheriff for County Wicklow. He became interested in a new political movement called the Home Rule League which was campaigning for a moderate degree of self-government for Ireland, as opposed to other movements which advocated total independence.

In 1875 he was elected to the British House of Commons as an MP under the Home Rule League banner, representing County Meath.

During his first year at the House of Commons he displayed a somewhat reserved disposition and for the most part remained silent and in the background.

However, after that initial period as a novice he quickly came to prominence as a strident and capable advocate of Irish nationalist issues.

He was frustrated at the lack of interest on the part of the British political establishment in Irish affairs and he resolved to effect change in that attitude.

He, along with his colleagues, embarked on a policy of 'obstructionism' in the House of Commons, in which they used technical procedures to frustrate the legislature and undermine its ability to function. This policy was very successful and projected Parnell into public prominence and also forced the British political establishment to address the 'Irish Issue'.

Parnell, at this time, was respected by the Irish and British politicians as a brilliant tactician, analyst and political organiser.

In 1879 he was elected president of the newly founded Irish National Land League. He engaged in a highly successful tour of America the same year, meeting with influential Irish Americans and collecting large amounts of money for the relief of distress in Ireland.

In 1880 he was elected leader of the Irish Party - a broad nationalist coalition of supporters of the Land League and moderate Fenians. He addressed large meetings throughout Ireland, advocating land reform. He supported William Gladstone, the Liberal leader, in the 1880 British elections. In those elections Parnell supporters and the Home Rule candidates enjoyed an astounding success.

When Gladstone introduced the Land Law (Ireland) Act 1881 it fell far short of Parnell's expectations and he withdrew his support for Gladstone and joined the Opposition benches.

In addition to parliamentary disruption, Parnell advocated the boycotting of English goods and he urged Irish farmers to refuse to cooperate with, or work for, English landlords. As a result of the success of the boycott campaign the Land League was suppressed and Gladstone introduced the Protection of Person and Property Act, 1881, which permitted imprisonment without trial and Parnell was arrested and taken to Kilmainham Gaol. This of course, enhanced his reputation greatly among his followers.

Parnell was released from Kilmainham Gaol in 1882 and he continued to campaign vigorously for Irish tenant rights and Home Rule. The Home Rule movement, and the 'Irish Cause' in general, was dealt a severe blow when two senior British officials were brutally murdered in Phoenix Park, Dublin in May 1882.

Parnell was shaken by this violence and the result was a closer working relationship with Gladstone in order to try to settle the 'Irish Question' in a non-violent manner.

In 1887 The Times newspaper revealed that it had evidence that Parnell condoned the Phoenix Park murders and that his followers had been involved. This caused uproar throughout Ireland and Britain and Parnell vehemently denied the allegations. He demanded that a Commission

Avondale House, Wicklow

of Enquiry be held, and this commission established conclusively in 1889 that the letters on which The Times based the accusations were forgeries.

This was the pinnacle of Parnell's career. When Parnell entered the House of Commons in 1890 after he had been cleared, he received a standing ovation from his fellow MP's, led by Gladstone.

It appeared that he could do no wrong - he was truly the

Contemporary sketch of Parnell addressing the House of Commons by James Lowther, MP

'uncrowned king of Ireland'. But in 1890 Parnell's career came crashing down around him, brought about not by any political issue, but by his private life.

He was implicated in divorce proceedings involving a Mrs. Katharine O'Shea.

Katharine ('Kitty') O'Shea (1846 - 1921) was born in Essex of aristocratic parents. She married Captain William O'Shea in 1867. Their marriage was an unhappy one.

When she and Parnell met in 1880 Kitty and her husband were already separated. They kept up a semblance of appearance and did not divorce because O'Shea was anticipating a substantial inheritance from one of Kitty's aunts and they were anxious not to jeopardise this.

Shortly after Parnell and Kitty met they settled into a highly domesticated relationship and didn't place too much emphasis on concealing it. They had three children together. It became the worst kept secret in London but nobody showed any concern about it. Captain O'Shea was well aware of it and it was believed that he actually condoned it in the expectation that it could do no harm to his own political career.

However, when the inheritance from Kitty's aunt didn't materialise, Captain O'Shea filed for divorce in 1889, citing Parnell as the co-respondent. Parnell assured the Irish Party that he would be exonerated and throughout 1890 resolutions of confidence in his leadership were passed at meetings throughout Ireland.

Parnell's feelings for Kitty were very strong, so much so that he didn't contest the divorce proceedings to ensure that the divorce would be granted and that he could then marry his beloved.

Even when the divorce was granted in 1890 there was little apparent unrest among his followers. Gladstone, however, issued a letter, addressed to Parnell, declaring that if Parnell didn't resign as leader of the Irish Party their alliance was finished and so were all prospects of Home Rule.

A special meeting of the parliamentary members of the Irish Party was held on December 1st to discuss the continuation of Parnell as their leader. Opinions were divided and sentiment was very strong on both sides. The result was that 44 out of the 73 members present walked out of the meeting and split with the Irish Party, leaving only 28 loyal supporters with Parnell.

The bitter split in the party was reflected among the ordinary people throughout Ireland and tore the country apart for decades.

In spite of the turmoil around him, Parnell married his beloved Kitty in June 1891 in Steyning Registry Office, having first unsuccessfully sought permission for a church wedding. They took up residence in Brighton.

He fought a long and fierce campaign to resurrect his former support in Ireland but was rejected by those very people whose interests he had championed for so many years.

Following a rigorous election tour in Ireland he died, dejected and disillusioned, at his home in Brighton on October 6th, 1891 at the age of forty-five. An estimated crowd of 200,000 people attended his funeral in Dublin. Such was his reputation that his gravestone of unhewn Wicklow granite carries just one word in large letters - PARNELL.

Kitty O'Shea lived the rest of her life in relative obscurity, an isolated and increasingly impecunious figure. She is buried in Littlehampton, Sussex, England.

Mrs. Katharine Parnell

**She Moved Through The Fair**

This song appears in the collection "Irish Country Songs" (1909) edited by the collector, Herbert Hughes, where he states that the melody originated in County Donegal, in the north-west of Ireland. It is a very well know and haunting love song.

The lyrics are by the Irish writer, Pádraic Colum (1881-1972).

Colum, in a radio interview, tells how Hughes approached him one day with a copy of the melody. There was nothing left of the lyrics but the last two lines. Colum then went about constructing lyrics which would suit the atmosphere of the song. He captured the sentiments perfectly.

Colum was born in County Longford and emigrated to the United States in 1914. One of his best-known works is the poem "An

Old Woman Of The Roads"

Herbert Hughes sets the song to a 6/4 timing, changing to 9/4 in places. However, the version I know has a 4/4 timing but it doesn't really adhere to a strict tempo and should be sung 'rubato' - without conforming to the given rhythm.

The ballad was sung by Sinéad O'Connor to great effect in the film "Michael Collins".

There is also a lovely version by the Breton harpist Alan Stivell on his album "Chemin de Terre".

The song is reproduced here by kind permission of the Estate of Pádraic Colum.

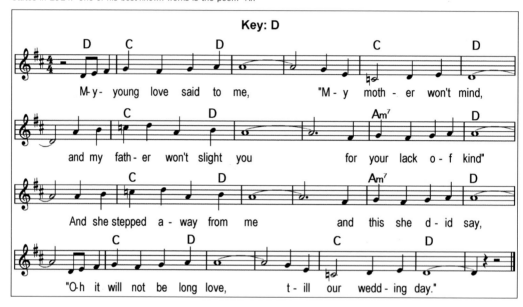

She went away from me and she moved through the fair
And fondly I watched her move here and move there
And she made her way homeward with one star awake
As the swan in the evening moves over the lake

The people were saying that no two were e'er wed
But one has a sorrow that never was said
And I smiled as she passed with her goods and her gear
And that was the last that I saw of my dear

Last night I did dream that my love she came in
And so softly she came that her feet made no din
And she laid her hand on me and smiling did say
"It will not be long love, till our wedding day"

Westport, Mayo

This is also known as "The Rose Of Allandale" and was written by
Sidney Nelson and Charles Jefferys.
Three different publications of the song are held in the Lester S.
Levy Collection of Sheet Music at the Sheridan Libraries of the
John Hopkins University, Maryland, USA.

This song didn't originate in Ireland but has been adopted by the
native population, mainly due to versions of the song recorded
by two of Ireland's best known singers, Paddy Reilly and Mary
Black.

Where e'er I wandered, east or west; though fate began to lour
A solace still she was to me in sorrow's lonely hour
When tempests lashed our lonesome barque and tore her shiv'ring sail
One maiden form withstood the storm; 'twas the Rose of Allendale
*Chorus*

And when my fevered lips were parched on Africa's hot sands
She whispered hopes of happiness and tales of distant lands
My life has been a wilderness, unblessed by fortune's gale
Had fate not linked my lot to hers, the Rose of Allendale
*Chorus*

**The Rose Of Mooncoin**

*(Verses and chorus have the same melody)*

This is the county anthem of all Kilkenny people worldwide and is sung with vigour at all GAA hurling matches whenever the Kilkenny team are playing.

Mooncoin is a small Kilkenny village situated beside the River Suir, about 8 miles from Waterford City on the main Waterford to Clonmel road.

The song was written by a local teacher, Watt Murphy, in the early 19th century. Watt fell madly in love with the daughter of the local rector. Her name was Elizabeth but she was also known as Molly. Watt and Molly would spend many's an evening walking along the banks of the Suir, reading and reciting poetry together. When the rector learned of this liaison he was not happy and he sent his daughter to England. Matt, heartbroken, wrote this song in her memory.

County Kilkenny, the ancient Kingdom of Ossory, has two river boundaries - the River Suir on the south-west and the River Barrow to the south-east. A third large river, the Nore, flows through the centre of the county in a pleasant wooded valley and joins the River Barrow near the point where it begins to widen into its long estuary. On the borders there is some high ground, notably the Slieveardagh and Booley Hills on the County Tipperary border and the hills around Graiguenemenegh near the River Barrow.

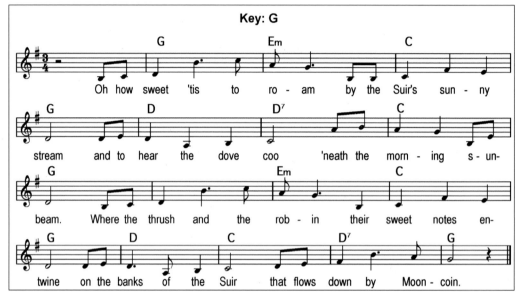

*Flow on lovely river, flow gently along*
*By your waters so sweet sounds the lark's merry song*
*On your green banks I'll wander where first I did join*
*With you, lovely Molly, the Rose of Mooncoin*

Oh Molly, dear Molly, it breaks my fond heart
To know that we shortly forever must part
I'll think of you Molly while sun and moon shine
On the banks of the Suir that flows down by Mooncoin
*Chorus*

She has sailed far away o'er the dark rolling foam
Far away from the hills of her dear Irish home
Where the fisherman sports with his small boat and line
By the banks of the Suir that flows down by Mooncoin
*Chorus*

Oh then here's to the Suir with its valleys so fair
Where oft times we wandered in the cool morning air
Where the roses are blooming and the lilies entwine
On the banks of the Suir that flows down by Mooncoin
*Chorus*

Mooncoin, Kilkenny

**Maids When You're Young**

*(Verses and chorus have the same melody)*

This bawdy ballad is well known in Ireland, England, Scotland and North America. It first appeared in 1869 in a collection of ballads by David Herd called "Ancient Scottish Songs, Heroic Ballads, etc." and in it the song was entitled "Scant Of Love, Want Of Love"

"Courting" is a quaint Irish verb which means, in its broadest sense, to "get romantically involved with". It would cover every activity from holding hands, to gentle kissing, to a whole lot of other things!

*For he's got no folurum fol diddle-i-urum da*
*He's got no folurum fol diddle-i-aye*
*He's got no flurum, he's lost his ding-durum da*
*Maids when you're young never wed an auld man*

When we went to church, hey ding-durum da
When we went to church me being young
When we went to church he left me in the lurch
Maids when you're young never wed an auld man
*Chorus*

When we went to bed, hey ding-durum da
When we went to bed me being young
When we went to bed he lay like he was dead
Maids when you're young never wed an auld man
*Chorus*

I threw my leg over him hey ding-durum da
I threw my leg over him me being young
I threw my leg over him, damn nearly smothered him
Maids when you're young never wed an auld man
*Chorus*

When he went to sleep, hey ding-durum da
When he went to sleep me being young
When he went to sleep out of bed I did creep
Into the arms of a willing young man
*Chorus change:- "And I found his falurum, fol diddle-i-urum da", etc.*

The earliest printed version of this ballad is in 1787 in "The Scots Musical Museum" published by the collector James Johnson. It was printed under the title "Lord Ronald, My Son".

It also appears in Francis J. Child's five volume work "The English and Scottish Popular Ballads" (1882 - 1898) under the name of "Lord Rendal".

This ballad is found throughout Ireland, Britain and North America and is also known as "Lord Randall", "Jimmy Randal" and "Jimmy Randolph".

It has been suggested that this song is associated with the death of Thomas Randolph (Randal) Earl of Moray who died in 1332. Speculation has it that he may have been poisoned by his wife. There's a German version, "Grossmutter-Schlangenkoechin", where the boy dies following a bite from a poisonous snake.

The melody has also been found in many countries on the European mainland.

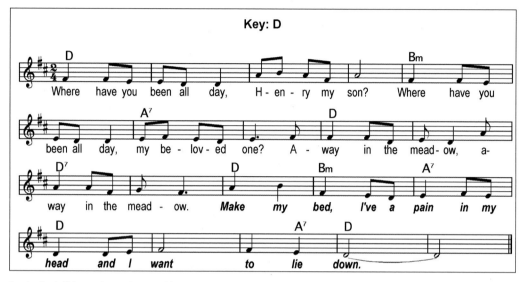

**Key: D**

Where have you been all day, H-en-ry my son? Where have you been all day, my be-lov-ed one? A-way in the mead-ow, a-way in the mead-ow. *Make my bed, I've a pain in my head and I want to lie down.*

And what did you have to eat, Henry my son
What did you have to eat, my beloved one
Poisoned beads, poisoned beads
*Chorus*

What colour were those beads, Henry my son
What colour were those beads, my beloved one
Green and yellow, green and yellow
*Chorus*

What will you leave your mother, Henry my son
What will you leave your mother, my beloved one
A woollen blanket, a woollen blanket
*Chorus*

What will you leave your children, Henry my son
What will you leave your children, my beloved one
The keys of heaven, the keys of heaven
*Chorus*

And what will you leave your sweetheart, Henry my son
What will you leave your sweetheart, my beloved one
A rope to hang her, a rope to hang her
*Chorus*

Wind-swept bushes, West of Ireland

Galway Bay from Oranmore, with the ruined 17th century De Burgh castle in the foreground

*(Verses and chorus have the same melody)*

A shawl is a type of loose cloak usually worn over the head and shoulders by peasant women.

The Galway Shawl has become part of Irish culture and has been worn since the early 1800's. It was traditionally worn by the women of the Claddagh district of Galway city and it was a most useful item of clothing, being used as a wrap, a bed cover and also as a piece of 'luggage' for carrying belongings on long journeys.

Oranmore is a small rural town to the east of Galway city which lies at the head of Oranmore Bay, a creek of the larger Galway Bay, and is situated at the western extremity of the plain which covers central Ireland between Dublin and Galway.

The names of some well-known polkas, reels and hornpipes are mentioned in the song.

Donegal is the most north-westerly county in Ireland.

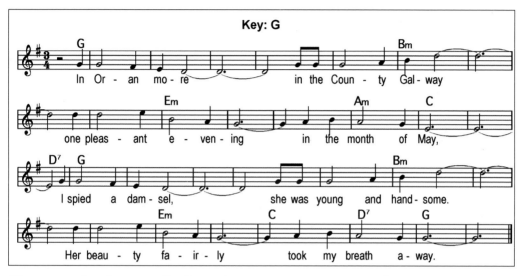

*She wore no jewels, no costly diamonds*
*No paint nor powder, no none at all*
*She wore a bonnet with a ribbon on it*
*And around her shoulders was a Galway shawl*

As we kept on walking she kept on talking
Till her father's cottage came into view
She said "Come in sir, and meet my father
And for to please him play 'The Foggy Dew'"
*Chorus*

I played 'The Blackbird' and 'The Stack of Barley'
'Rodney's Glory' and 'The Foggy Dew'
She sang each note like an Irish linnet
And the tears they flowed in her eyes of blue
*Chorus*

'Twas early, early, all in the morning
I hit the road for old Donegal
She said "Goodbye sir" and her eyes seemed brighter
And my heart remained with the Galway shawl
*Chorus*

**A Bunch Of Thyme**

This ballad has been traced back as far as the 17th century and versions can be found in Ireland and Britain.
It was a major hit for the Irish folk duo, Foster & Allen and reached no. 18 in the UK Charts in February 1982.

"Thyme" in this ballad is a reference to innocence and virginity and the ballad suggests that you should never trust a sailor!
The song was recorded by Christy Moore on his album "Whatever Tickles Your Fancy" (1975).

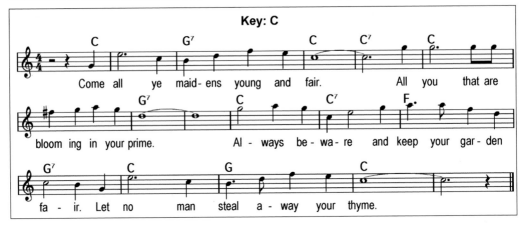

For thyme, it is a precious thing
And thyme brings all things to my mind
Thyme with all its flavours, along with all its joys
Thyme brings all things to my mind

Once I had a bunch of thyme
I thought it never would decay
Then came a lusty sailor who chanced to pass my way
He stole my bunch of thyme away

The sailor gave to me a rose
A rose that never would decay
He gave it to me, to keep me reminded
Of when he stole my thyme away

*(Repeat first verse)*

Dingle Peninsula, Kerry

This old ballad has a question-and-answer pattern which is often found with older types of Anglo-Scots 'riddling' ballads. There is an old Scots ballad entitled 'The Trooper And The Maid' with a very similar theme and lyrics.

My two favourite versions of this ballad are by the traditional group Planxty on their CD "Planxty" and also by The Woods Band on their album "The Woods Band" (1971).

Key: Em

Who are you me pret-ty fa-ir maid. Who are you me dar - ling.

Who are you, me pret-ty fa-ir maid. Who are you me dar - ling. And she

ans-wered me qui-te mod-est-ly "I am me moth-er's dar-ling". **With me**

too-ry-a, fol de did-dle da, Di-re fol de did-dle dair-re-e oh.

"And will you come to my mother's house when the moon is shining clearly *(repeat)*
I'll open the door and I'll let you in and divil the one will hear us". **Chorus**

So I went to her house in the middle of the night when the moon was shining clearly *(repeat)*
And she opened the door and she let me in and divil the one did hear us. **Chorus**

She took my horse by the bridle and the bit and she led him to the stable *(repeat)*
Saying "There's plenty of oats for a soldier's horse to eat them if he's able". **Chorus**

Then she took me by the lily-white hand and she led me to the table *(repeat)*
Saying "There's plenty of wine for the soldier boy to drink it if your able". **Chorus**

I got up and I made me bed and I made it nice and easy *(repeat)*
Then I took her up and I laid her down saying "Lassie are you able?" **Chorus**

And there we lay till the breaking of the day and divil the one did hear us *(repeat)*
Then I arose and put on my clothes, saying "Lassie, I must leave you". **Chorus**

"And when will you return again and when will we be married?" *(repeat)*
"When broken shells make Christmas bells, then will we be married". **Chorus**

# James Joyce and Nora Barnacle

James Joyce (1882 - 1941) is considered to be one of Ireland's greatest literary figures and his reputation as a literary genius is worldwide.

He was born James Augustine Joyce in 1882 at Brighton Square in the middle-class south Dublin suburb of Rathgar.

His parents were John Joyce, who was working in the office of the collector of rates for Dublin at the time of Joyce's birth, and Mary (May) Murray.

When Joyce was about ten years old his father ran into financial difficulties and was drinking heavily. With so many mouths to feed this quickly led to financial ruin for the Joyce family. Unable to pay the rent bills, the Joyces moved to an extraordinary number of addresses in Dublin, each one more rundown than the preceding one.

John Joyce lost his position in the rate collector's office in 1891 and eked out a survival on his small pension and occasional odd jobs. Notwithstanding the financial difficulties, Joyce managed to obtain an excellent education and in 1898 attended University College Dublin.

His manner was that of a very confident individual who was unaffected by what other people thought of him. His early sexual life was in the company of prostitutes for which he would immediately be repentent. He was a reticent student who could show great wit at times. When under the influence of alcohol he could be boisterous and crude.

He graduated with a Bachelor of Arts degree in 1902 and took up medical studies in Dublin. Unhappy with the way his studies were progressing in Dublin, he decided to move to medical school in Paris.

His activities in Paris were curtailed when his mother took ill and he returned to Dublin in 1903. His mother died of liver cancer in August of that year.

The Joyce family's financial difficulties deteriorated even further at this time and Joyce tried his hand at several different jobs without great success. He moved into a converted Martello Tower in the south Dublin suburb of Sandycove and shared it with a Dublin medical student, Oliver St. John Gogarty.

Around this time, on June 10th 1904, one of the most important events in Joyce's life occurred. He chanced to strike up a conversation with a good-looking girl in Nassau Street. Her name was Nora Barnacle.

Nora Barnacle (1884 - 1951) was born in Galway City. She had a difficult upbringing. Her father, a baker, was a heavy drinker and her mother struggled to keep her large family together.

Nora left school at thirteen to take up a series of menial positions. She left Galway in 1904 and took up a position as a chambermaid at Finn's Hotel in Nassau Street, Dublin.

She was walking along Nassau Street on June 10th when a young man wearing a sailor's cap struck up conversation with her. It was James Joyce. The conversation ended with them both agreeing to meet in front of the Wilde's house on the corner of Merrion Square on June 14th.

Nora, however, stood Joyce up and never appeared. The dejected Joyce sent a note to her, asking her to meet with him. An appointment was made for the evening of June 16th and they both went walking around Ringsend, and they agreed to meet again.

Joyce enshrines that fateful day in literary history by using it - June 16th 1904 - as the day in which the events of his famous novel, 'Ulysses', take place. By doing this, he is telling the world, and Nora, of the importance he holds for that encounter. It's an everlasting tribute to their relationship and forever etched in history and now recognised universally as 'Bloomsday'.

The friendship of the young couple intensified during the summer of that year and through his prolific correspondence with her it becomes clear that he is deeply in love with her.

To anybody else with Joyce's intellect and education, Nora would have appeared 'rough around the edges' - spirited, witty, earthy, but uneducated and lacking any interest in the arts or literature. But Joyce was attracted to her and in those summer months of 1904 he was experiencing feelings that he had never felt before - feelings he couldn't ignore.

By the autumn of 1904 Joyce had become disillusioned with his existence in Dublin and he asked Nora to elope with him and leave Ireland. Even though she had met him less than four months previously she agreed.

The couple departed Ireland en route to Zurich, where Joyce had been promised a language teaching position. They were dismayed to learn that the particular job did not exist. They then travelled onwards to Trieste and Joyce finally obtained a position in Pula, in Austro-Hungary, now part of Croatia.

During this period he was writing constantly with some degree of success, but without any accompanying financial success. As Joyce's jobs ebbed and flowed they were regularly moving home. The birth of their son, George, in 1905 introduced an element of stability into their lives but Nora still had to deal with Joyce's heavy drinking. She coped well under the pressure of his volatile creative disposition and their financial uncertainty.

They travelled yet farther in an attempt to find greater financial stability and Nora gave birth to their daughter, Lucia, in 1907.

Notwithstanding their financial and material difficulties the family coped well and Joyce and Nora were very much in love.

In 1909, however, a crisis arose which shook their

relationship to its foundations. While on one of his rare visits to Dublin Joyce was informed by one of his former college classmates, Vincent Cosgrave, that he had also been 'walking out' with Nora in 1904 during the time that Joyce was courting her and writing graphic and passionate love letters to her.

Joyce was devastated and wrote several letters in succession to Nora seeking the truth of the matter, not wishing to believe Cosgrave's story. He called on another former classmate and close friend, John Francis Byrne, to discuss the matter. He was in such a state when he called to Byrne that Byrne wrote later that he had never seen a human being more shattered.

Byrne managed to persuade him that the utterance of Cosgrave was a complete lie and he now needed to make amends with Nora for his assumptions that she had been unfaithful to him.

This episode strengthened their relationship and increased the depth of feelings they had for each other. As the couple entered middle-age their lives gradually settled down. In 1921 they moved to Paris where they lived for almost twenty years. At this time, Joyce was receiving greater recognition for his work and this led to less financial instability for the family.

Throughout all of their time together, up to this point they were not married - a sign of Joyce's disdain for organised religion. However, on July 4th, 1931 the couple were legally married in an English registry office - 27 years after they first met. He was 49, she 47.

They returned to Paris after the marriage and in December 1940 they moved to Zurich. On January 13th 1941 Joyce died, leaving Nora alone for the first time in almost forty years.

It is impossible to calculate the impact that Nora had over the artistic and personal life of her genius husband. There was no doubt but that Joyce was a difficult man to live with but he adored his wife and this is quite evident both in the living of their lives together and their copious correspondence.

Nora's love and affection for Joyce, as a man and not an artist, was clearly one of the important foundations of their relationship and must have helped to sustain Joyce through many of the difficult periods of his life and work.

Nora died in Zurich on April 10th 1951. There was not enough space at Fluntern Cemetery for her to be buried next to her husband.

In 1966 they were reburied next to each other - together again in death as they had been for most of their lives.

The Joyces in London on their wedding day, July 4th 1931.

Courtesy of The Poetry Collection, The State University of New York at Buffalo

75

This ballad has often been referred to as "The Derry Air" or, more politically and geographically correct, "The Londonderry Air". However, as there are over 100 songs composed to the melody it's more correct to call it "Danny Boy". (Thomas Moore composed a song to this melody, called "My Gentle Harp".)

This is undoubtedly one of the most popular ballads to be heard in the kitchens and pubs of Ireland!

It is also one of the most consistently murdered ballads I know, because amateur balladeers usually start singing it in a pitch too high for their voice and then realising (when it is too late!) that they can't reach the high E note towards the end of the verse. Keep that in mind - don't get caught out!

The melody first appeared in print in "Ancient Music of Ireland" (1855) by the collector George Petrie in which he gratefully thanks a Miss Jane Ross of Newtown-Limavady in County Derry (Northern Ireland) for bringing the song to his attention. He also states that "the name of the tune unfortunately was not ascertained by Miss Ross, who sent it to me with the simple remark that it was 'very old', in the correctness of which statement I have no hesitation in expressing my perfect

concurrence". Thus it was baptised "The Derry Air".

However as no other versions of the melody were ever reported by any of the other folk music collectors there is speculation that Miss Ross may have composed the air herself but for some reason didn't wish to claim credit for it. The speculation still continues to the present day.

The lyrics of Danny Boy were written by an English lawyer, Frederic Edward Weatherly (1848 - 1929). In 1910 he wrote the lyrics and music for an unsuccessful song he called 'Danny Boy'. However in 1912 his sister-in-law sent him the score of 'The Derry Air' from America and he immediately noticed that his Danny Boy lyrics perfectly fitted the melody.

In 1913 he published the song in its new form.

Danny Boy is recognised worldwide as one of Ireland's greatest anthems and has been recorded on hundreds of different occasions by such artists as Mario Lanza, Judy Garland, The Pogues, Bing Crosby and The Mormon Tabernacle Choir.

One of the best versions is to be found on The Chieftans album "Tears Of Stone" (1999) on which the song is sung by the Canadian jazz singer Diana Krall.

And when ye come and all the flowers are dying
And if I'm dead, as dead I well may be
You'll come and find the place where I am lying
And kneel and say an 'Avé' there for me
And I shall hear, though soft you tread above me
And all my grave will warmer, sweeter be
If you will bend and tell me that you love me
Then I shall sleep in peace until you're here with me

Clare Island

Dunmanus Bay, West Cork

This song dates back to the 17th Century and is well known throughout England, Scotland and Ireland.
It also goes under the name of "The False Bride" or "The Week Before Easter".

The late Sandy Denny, former lead singer with Fairport Convention, recorded this song for an album entitled "Alex Campbell and His Friends" in 1967. It was later reissued on an album entitled "The Original Sandy Denny" in 1978.

**Key: G**

I once loved a lass and I loved her so well that I ha-ted all oth-ers that spoke of her ill. But now she's re-ward-ed me well for my love for she's gone to be wed with an-oth-er.

When I saw my love walk through the church door
With groom and bride maidens they made a fine show
And I followed them in with my heart full of woe
For now she is wed to another

When I saw my love sit down for to dine
I sat down beside her and poured out the wine
I drank to the lassie that should have been mine
But now she is wed to another

The men in yon forest, they ask it of me
How many strawberries grow in the salt sea?
And I ask of them back with a tear in my eye
How many ships sail in the forest?

So dig me a grave and dig it so deep
And cover me over with flowers so sweet
And I will turn in for to take a long sleep
And maybe in time I'll forget her

They dug him a grave and they dug it so deep
They covered him over with flowers so sweet
And he has turned in for to take a long sleep
And maybe by now he's forgotten

Muckross House and Gardens, Killarney, Kerry

**The Banks Of Claudy**

In 1898 a collector of folk songs, Kate Lee, came across a ballad in East Sussex called "Claudy Banks" in which the lovers were called Betsy and Johnny. Many other similar versions of this song exist where the girl's name changes to Betty, Patsy or Nancy, and the boy's name to William.

I boldly stepped up to her, I took her by surprise
I own she did not know me, I being dressed in disguise
"Where are you going my fair one, my joy and heart's delight
Where are you going to wander this cold and windy night?"

"It's on the way to Claudy's banks, if you will please to show
Take pity on a stranger, for there I want to go
It's seven long years or better since Johnny has left this shore
He's crossing the wide ocean, where the foaming billows roar"

"He's crossing the wide ocean for honour and for fame
His ship's been wrecked so I've been told down on the Spanish Main"
"It's on the Banks of Claudy fair maiden whereon you stand
Now don't you believe young Johnny, for he's a false young man"

Now when she heard this dreadful news she fell into despair
For the wringing of her tender hands and the tearing of her hair
"If Johnny he be drowned no man alive I'll take
Through lonesome glens and valleys I'll wander for his sake"

Now when he saw her loyalty no longer could he stand
He fell into her arms saying "Betsy I'm the man".
Saying "Betsy I'm the young man who caused you all the pain,
And since we've met on Claudy's banks we'll never part again"

*(Verses and chorus have the same melody)*

It is thought that this old ballad may have originated in Belfast. Some versions of the song begin with the lines "In a neat little town they call Belfast".

The first known printed version was contained in "Folk Songs From Hampshire" (1909) edited by George Gardiner.

This very popular Irish ballad carries with it a stern warning about never trusting the fairer sex!

Many Irish men and women were deported, or 'transported' to Van Diemen's Land (originally referring to Tasmania, but the name was later used colloquially to refer to Australia itself) by the British authorities during the 19th century - often for very petty crimes.

Tasmanian whalers also have a song similar to this one called "The Hat With The Velvet Band".

"Kilkenny" city is in central Ireland, and is the capital of County Kilkenny.

The Irish Ballad Group The Dubliners reached No. 15 in the UK Singles Charts with this song in August 1967.

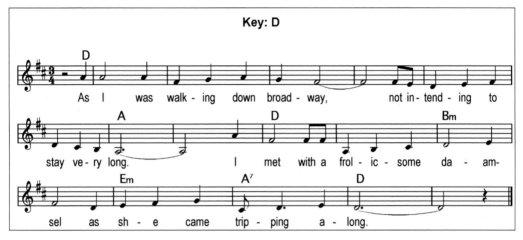

Key: D

As I was walk-ing down broad-way, not in-tend-ing to stay ve-ry long. I met with a frol-ic-some da-am-sel as sh-e came trip-ping a-long.

A gold watch she took out of her pocket and placed it right into my hand
On the very first time that I saw her; bad luck to the black velvet band

*Her eyes they shone like diamonds; you'd think she was queen of the land*
*With her hair thrown over her shoulder; tied up with a black velvet band*

'Twas in the town of Kilkenny; an apprentice to trade I was bound
With gaiety and bright amusement to see all the days go around
Till misfortune and trouble came over me which forced me to stray from the land
Far away from my friends and relations; betrayed by the black velvet band
*Chorus*

Before judge and jury next morning the both of us did appear
A gentleman swore to his jewellery and the case against us was clear
Seven long years' transportation away down to Van Diemen's Land
Far away from my friends and relations to follow the black velvet band
*Chorus*

Now all you brave young Irish lads a warning please gather from me
Beware of the pretty young damsels you meet all around Kilkenny
They'll treat you with whiskey and porter until you're unable to stand
And before you have time for to leave them you'll be sent down to Van Diemen's Land
*Chorus*

**Peggy Gordon**

This ballad doesn't appear to have originated in Ireland and is more likely to have its roots in either Scotland or Canada.
A version of it was recorded by the popular Scottish folk group, The Corries, and in Ireland by Luke Kelly and The Dubliners.
There is no record of any location called Ingo and the theory is that it could be a shortened or slang version of England.
In the US Library of Congress 'Music For The Nation' section

there are historical records of a song called "Sweet Maggie Gordon", published by a Mrs. Pauline Lieder in New York in 1880, and arranged by Mr. Ned Straight.
"Sweet Maggie Gordon", has a chorus very similar to this song, whereas some of the verses bear a remarkable resemblance to the well-known Irish ballad "Carrickfergus" (page 2)

I'm so in love and I can't deny it
My heart is smothered in my breast
It's not for you to let the world know it
A troubled mind sure it knows no rest

I put my head to a glass of brandy
It is my fancy I do declare
For when I'm drinking I'm always thinking
And wishing Peggy Gordon was here

I wish I was away in Ingo
Far across the briny sea
Sailing o'er the deepest ocean
Where love nor care never bothered me

I wish I was in some lonesome valley
Where womankind could not be found
Where little birds sing in the branches
And every moment a different sound

*(Repeat the first verse)*

*(Note that four of the 'C' chords should by played slightly before the relevant note - as per the score)*

Cliffs of Moher, Clare

**Removal of CD**

Carefully cut a slit in the CD sleeve to remove the CD from the CD case.
Your CD can be stored in this CD sleeve, which is permanently fixed to this book cover so that you can keep it safely with the book at all times.
Do not attempt to remove this CD case from the cover of the book as it will result in damage to the book.

www.greatirishballads.com